Keeping it Real!

Keeping it Real!
7 Steps Toward a Healthier You
A Biblical Resource for Women

Gloria Morrow, Ph.D.

Shining Glory Publications, Inc.
Pomona, California

Published by Shining Glory Publications, Inc.
2249 North Garey Avenue
Pomona, California 91767
(909) 392-6907

Notice: The information in this book is true and complete to the best of the author and publisher's knowledge. However, the names and other pertinent details concerning individuals in this book have been changed. This book is intended only as a study guide and should not replace, countermand, or conflict with the advice given to readers by their professional mental health providers, and/or physicians. It is sold with the understanding that the author and publisher are not engaged in rendering medical, mental health, psychological, or any other kind of personal or professional services in the book. The reader should consult her or his culturally competent medical and/or mental health professional before adopting any of the suggestions in this book or drawing inferences from it. The author and publisher disclaim all liability in connection with the specific personal use of any and all information provided in this book.

Morrow, Gloria, 1950-
        Keeping it Real! 7 steps toward a healthier you/by Gloria Morrow.
-1st ed. P.cm.

Library of Congress Control Number: 2003115310

ISBN 0-9747168-6-3

Printed and bound in the United States of America

This book is dedicated to all the women in my life; especially my mother Henrietta Phillips. I would not know the importance of good health, without your profound wisdom and example.
To my daughters, Sharmika, TaMia, TaLese, and my beloved granddaughter, MaLaun, may each of you live your life like its golden!

Keeping it Real!

Contents

Foreword

From a very young age, I had a real love and passion for music. My dad would take us all over Oklahoma, and surrounding cities to sing. I was also very smart in school, and I had big plans for a great music career and future. While my parents had high hopes for me too, the Great Depression and other life circumstances prevented me from pursuing my goals when I wanted to, and I became very disappointed. That disappointment turned into sadness.

It took many years of walking with the Lord and wise counsel to help me to overcome that disappointment so I could really pursue my purpose with passion. I initially thought I was called to become a concert pianist, but God had another plan. His plan was bigger than mine, and He called me to teach others how to play the piano, a calling I have enjoyed for the past 50 years. I had to wait until I became an adult to fulfill the passion God birthed in me, but I learned a long time ago that God is in total control of my life.

Unfortunately, many women have given up because they have allowed disappointment and pains of the past to prevent them from living a healthy and fulfilled life. It is never too late for you to walk in your destiny.

Dr. Gloria Morrow has written an excellent Biblically based book entitled, *Keeping it Real! 7 Steps Toward a Healthier You.* This book has been written to help women to become healthier in every area of their lives. I highly recommend that you read it and apply it to your lives. ***Keeping it Real! 7 Steps Toward a Healthier You*** will assist you in developing a healthier mind, body, and Spirit. It may be difficult to confront your core issues as you read the pages of this wonderful book, but it is necessary for healing. God will walk with you every step of the way.

Trust in the Lord with all your heart,
and lean not on your own understanding;
In all your ways acknowledge Him,
and He shall direct your paths. Proverbs 3:5-6 NKJV

- Henrietta Phillips

Acknowledgements

I would like to take this opportunity to thank my husband and pastor, Reverend Tommy Morrow and our son, Steven (S.P.) for all your assistance on this project. Without your love, support, encouragement, and advice, this project would have been impossible. I thank and praise God for you.

Everyday of my life I am thankful to my parents, Reverend Harold and Henrietta Phillips for walking with me through all those dark days. God demonstrated His unconditional love and acceptance through you, and for that I will be eternally grateful. Mom, thank you for that beautiful foreword. No one, except God, knows my heart better than you.

I would also like to thank my personal assistant, Sharmika Phillips, and armor bearers, Annie Washington, Joella Washington, Joann Washington, and Phyllis Phelps for all your assistance to me as I minister and share with ladies all across the country. Your spiritual gifts and talents are highly appreciated and I thank God that you have accepted the call to serve. A special thanks to my Victory family, especially Ms. Essie Coleman who reminds us every Sunday to *Keep it Real*. To my editor Tom Marshall, thank you for your critical eye and assistance to me on this project.

Lastly, I would like to thank all the women who have allowed me to share the ministry of healing with you. It is my prayer that as you continue to experience God's healing and deliverance, you will walk in your calling, and allow God to use you in spectacular ways for the building of His Kingdom.

Introduction

It was a rainy day, and Wanda remembers having to force herself to get up and go to work. It was becoming increasingly difficult for her to get out of bed each day. Wanda's parents thought her consistent tardiness was due to her staying up late at night. No one knew that she was really suffering on the inside and on a downward spiral. Wanda also had difficulty sleeping at night, which explained her being tired almost every morning. So getting up in the morning was not simply a problem because she stayed up late at night. Wanda just wanted to sleep all day, which is a classic symptom of depression.

This day was different, however, because not only did she want to sleep all day, crazy thoughts were racing in her head. Wanda thought about all the mistakes she had made. She was tormented by errors in judgment, and the guilt was driving her out of her mind. Wanda looked in the mirror, and she hated what she saw. She did not like the picture staring back at her, and she felt worthless and hopeless. Wanda thought to herself, "I should be completing my second year of college." Then she remembered that every time attempts were made to start school, she would drop out before even starting. You see, Wanda did not think she was good enough, pretty enough, or smart enough.

Let me take a moment to set the story up properly. Wanda, the daughter of a pastor met and fell in love with an older guy who robbed her of her innocence at the age of 17 after a marriage proposal. She became pregnant after their first encounter. While her parents were very supportive and loving, Wanda's announcement was bittersweet. She was excited about the baby and she instantly developed love for her unborn child. But she began to realize that the baby's father was not the person she thought he was, and a wedding was out of the question.

Wanda became very angry and experienced feelings of betrayal because of his dishonesty. Further, Wanda was denied the opportunity of graduating with her class, forcing her to attend a special school for disabled students because of her condition. This news was the final straw in her cap of disappointment, and Wanda became preoccupied with guilt due to the belief that she had let everyone down including herself.

Her most disturbing thought was the belief that she had disappointed God. This thinking caused Wanda to become extremely hard on herself, and she began to see herself in a very negative light. After giving birth to a beautiful baby boy she loved and adored, and close to three years later, we see Wanda still struggling with the same guilt. It was eating away at her soul, causing her to experience a deep depression.

With all the negative thoughts clouding her mind, Wanda struggled to get ready for work because she could not miss any additional days. She had already been written up for excessive tardiness and absenteeism. That was not the first time Wanda struggled to get herself moving, but there was something very different about that day. She was irritable, and upon arriving to work she began to look for reasons to leave early. So it is not surprising that the negative thoughts grew more intense. Wanda went to a very dark place, and made the decision to look for something to soothe herself, perhaps permanently. She searched her purse, and bingo, there Wanda found a bottle of pills. She grabbed the pills hurriedly, as if to avoid changing her mind, and went into the bathroom to take herself out of her misery. Then Wanda did the unthinkable, she swallowed close to 20 pills.

She really thought it would be over soon, and as she sat in the bathroom stall waiting, Wanda had to force herself not to think about her young son, parents, siblings, and friends. She could not bear to think about the hurt and pain they would suffer because of her selfish actions. All Wanda knew, it would be over soon. But after staring at the pill bottle, she began to feel very nauseous and sick to her stomach. Wanda began to panic because she did not think that death would be painful. Then it clicked! This desperate young woman had ingested 20 antibiotics and not the painkillers she thought she was taking. Wanda became almost amused, yet frightened as she thought to herself, "I can't even accomplish the simple task of killing myself."

After being jolted into thinking about the reality of what she was trying to do, Wanda called her mother and explained her version of the story. "Mom, I ACCIDENTALLY ingested too many antibiotics," stated Wanda as she attempted to be lighthearted and comical, a strategy she routinely used to mask her pain. Her parents rushed her to the emergency room where Wanda experienced the painful process of getting her stomach pumped.

When most people look at Wanda, they would never guess she had ever attempted to take her own life in a moment of absolute despair and brokenness. But she, like so many others, wore a mask day after day in order to hide the broken person underneath the mask.

Can I keep it real? Wanda was me, and my personal story is an example of what can happen when one is unhealthy and severely broken. I was a Christian who went to church every Sunday. I even taught a Sunday school class and served as the musician at my father's church. But I had not recovered from past hurts and disappointments which contributed to how I saw myself.

Furthermore, the guilt I carried due to the mistakes of a naïve teenager with low self-esteem propelled me even further into a hole of despair. I suffered on the inside in silence, feeling isolated and alone because I did not think anyone could understand what I was thinking and feeling.

At first glance, my story may appear to be an extreme reaction to a painful past. I am convinced, however, that I am not the only one who has thought about or currently thinks about ending their life prematurely. Even if you would never think about harming yourself, perhaps you are self-destructive in other ways as far too many women are. In my work as a clinical psychologist, women from every walk of life are hurting and broken because of past experiences and trauma, and they tend to self-medicate with food, excessive spending, drugs, alcohol, illicit sexual behaviors, gambling, and overworking.

Broken women have a difficult time setting and reaching personal, professional, and spiritual goals, and maintaining healthy interpersonal relationships with spouses, children, family, and friends, and fail to live out the purpose that God has ordained for their lives. Basically, far too many of us in the faith community lead pretty unhealthy mental, physical, and spiritual lives, which may explain why we lack sufficient power to do the work of Christ. I shared my personal testimony to let you know that God can heal and deliver, no matter what you have been through.

After that experience in the emergency room, I realized that it was not God's timing for me to die, and He had an awesome plan for my life. I began to seek His face, and to build a stronger relationship with Him. But I also discovered that I needed to confront and deal with past issues and hurts as well as to forgive myself and others who had hurt me. Going through that process also required me to talk to a trained Biblically-based mental health professional to help me to deal with my depression and to live a healthier lifestyle. God uses people to help broken people, and He wanted me to be whole so I could fulfill the purpose He had for me. Now that is my mission and ministry.

In looking back, I now know that God was setting me up to work with broken people because I can certainly relate to the brokenness in others. I am finally able to use my testimony, together with a healthy relationship with God, Biblical preparation, and academic training to help others who are hurting. It was out of this compassion for ministering to the unique needs of women that God called and empowered me to develop a 7-week seminar series for women, entitled *Keeping it Real! 7 Steps Toward a Healthier You*, and this accompanying guide to healthy living.

  Keeping it Real! 7 Steps Toward a Healthier You, the book, is a Biblical tool to help broken women to begin their process of healing and deliverance. There are many books that provide wonderful strategies for healthy living, and *Keeping it Real! 7 Steps Toward a Healthier You* is simply another helpful resource that provides strategies that were helpful to me during my difficult process of healing. It was not easy to confront my issues, but it was necessary. Likewise, this journey will not be easy for some of you, because you may have grown accustomed to feeling that way. Well help is on the way!

  Throughout the pages of this book, I will share my own personal experiences, and the experiences of those I work with to help you through this process. Please note that their stories are fictionalized to protect their identity and to maintain confidentiality. In addition, some of the seminar participants have given permission for me to share some of their thoughts and reflections regarding this relevant and timely topic.

  Keeping it Real! 7 Steps Toward a Healthier You is for "Big Girls," those who are sick and tired of being sick and tired. This book has been written for those who are tired of living a defeated life, and those who are ready to fully participate in your healing process.

Keeping it Real! 7 Steps Toward a Healthier You is for those of you who realize that it is unhealthy to continue to hold everyone else responsible for your inability to move forward and progress in life. Remember, God wants to transform you from a victim to a victor.

Keeping it Real! 7 Steps Toward a Healthier You is also for those who are ready to allow God to take complete control over their lives. This will be impossible unless you have received Jesus Christ as your personal Lord and Savior. For those who have not received Jesus into your heart, please read this awesome promise of salvation found in Romans 10: 9-13:

That if you confess with your mouth the Lord Jesus, and believe in your heart that God has raised Him from the dead, you will be saved. For with the heart one believes unto righteousness, and with the mouth confession is made unto salvation. For the Scripture says, whosoever believes on Him shall not be put to shame. For there is no distinction between Jew and Greek, for the same Lord over all is rich to all who call upon Him. For whosoever calls on the name of the Lord shall be saved.

If you are ready to join the family of God, or if you previously joined and are not sure of your status with God, please pray this simple prayer:

Lord Jesus, I know that I am a sinner, and I realize that I cannot save myself. Lord please forgive me of all my sins, and receive me into your family, the body of Christ. I believe that you are the son of the living God, and that you died and rose again to set me free according to the Scripture. Thank you for saving me.

You have made a courageous and live-changing decision today. Now, it is important to find a Bible believing church where you can learn about God and grow as a Christian. It is also of importance for you to become assured of your salvation, which will come as you grow in the knowledge of Christ. Be sure to find a church that demonstrates love and nurturance, because you will need their love and support during this time in your life. Congratulations on your new journey, and welcome to the family of God. Today is your Spiritual birthday.

God is calling His daughters to become whole, and even though it may not be easy to do the necessary work toward your healing, it will be well worth it. Just remember, you will not go through the valley alone because God will walk with you every step of the way.

Their soul abhorred all manner of food, and they drew near to the gates of death. Then they cried out to the Lord in their trouble, and He saved them out of their distresses. He sent His word and healed them, and delivered them from their destructions. Oh that men would give thanks to the Lord for His goodness, and for His wonderful works to the children of men!

Psalms 107:18-21

Chapter One

Take Off the Mask
Even When it Hurts!

I could ask the darkness to hide me and the light around me to become

night-but even in darkness I cannot hide from you.

Psalms 139:11-12 NIV

I will never forget the day I decided that being somebody else was easier than confronting me and the issues that plagued me. I just could not handle what I was feeling on the inside, and I did not want others to know, so I pulled out the mask. Can I keep it real? I wore the people pleaser mask. I erroneously believed that being nice would help people to like and accept me. This strategy created more problems for me because it took a lot of hard work to try to please others all the time. It was very tiring. Furthermore, you can never fully please others, so I became easily frustrated by the lack of appreciation I received after all my hard work.

Well don't judge me so harshly, because I am not alone in using the cover-up strategy for dealing with pain. It is not easy to face one's own pain at times, and to avoid that process, some of you also wear a mask to cover it up. Initially, it appears that the mask is effective in camouflaging the real deal, but unfortunately, wearing it may keep one locked into a dark and isolated prison with the potential for the individual to live in bondage until something or someone sets the captive free.

It wasn't until I reached my lowest point that I was able to acknowledge my brokenness and give permission for the mask to be removed, which in my case was the first step toward my becoming healthy and whole. However, I could not do it alone. I needed help! I was in desperate need of inner healing and deliverance.

Nothing changed for me until I realized that in order for me to be healthy and to fulfill God's purpose for my life I had to seek help from the master healer and those He ordained to minister healing to me. But it was not easy for me to acknowledge my condition to anyone. I really thought I was successful in hiding and disguising the pain, and I was convinced that nobody knew. I even became good at hiding the anger that seemed to persist, especially when my efforts to please did not seem to validate me as I expected.

Nobody Knows

Dorothy served as the administrative assistant to the pastor for 14 years. She was responsible for taking care of the pastor's church and personal business, and assisting his wife and children when called upon to do so. Dorothy was the epitome of joy and happiness, and she always had a pleasant smile on her face when everyone was looking. Unfortunately, when this gentle woman of God was alone or away from her daily responsibilities she presented quite differently.

You see Dorothy lived with an alcoholic and abusive husband who called himself a Christian, but was missing in action from church and from God. After one of his many attempts to *deal* with her as he would affectionately call the abuse, Dorothy broke down one day in the church office. She was finally forced to speak to the pastor about what was going on in her home. The pastor was perplexed when he learned that Dorothy wore a beautiful mask day after day, Sunday after Sunday to hide what was going on in her personal world.

Dorothy is not alone! Many women who are actively involved in ministry lead secret lives outside the church. Whether the secret involves hidden brokenness or ungodly living, these women suffer on the inside in silence. It is God's desire that his daughters be whole in every area, but unfortunately, far too many of us continue to walk around wearing a mask of deception hoping that God and the general public will see the picture we want them to see. Can you identify with this saying, "You can run, but you can't hide? Well, you may be able to cover up your pain from the people around you, but you can't hide from God.

Spiritual Nuggets

In Psalms 139:1-18, what does David teach us about God's all-seeing eye?

Dorothy wore the mask because she did not want to expose the trauma in her life. She believed that covering up the pain would make it disappear. We are often taught from a very early age that whatever goes on in the home must stay in the home. Dorothy may have been uncomfortable about sharing her personal business because of what she had been taught.

A Word of Caution to the Saints

Some people have a difficult time discussing their inner turmoil because they do not have a safe place to go to share. The church should be that safe place. In some cases, however, there is the potential for well meaning or broken Saints to expose those things that have been shared in confidence. So to the Saints of God, please exercise confidentiality and care for one another or you may become guilty of contributing to the pain of those who entrusted you with their care.

> ## *Spiritual Nuggets*
> What instructions does God give to the believer in Galatians 6:1-10
> concerning how we are to treat one another?

Some wear a mask because it is too difficult to deal with their reality, causing them to deny their pain. Janice lived in that state of denial. She lived with and cared for a mother who suffered from serious and chronic mental illness. Janice was her mother's caretaker, and she rarely went out socially. Her routine was going to work, going to church, and taking care of her mother. She had little time for friends or social outings. While maintaining this routine, Janice walked around like everything was just fine. However, she was beginning to exhibit some of the signs to indicate that her life was unraveling, such as experiencing bad headaches and stomach pain, loss of appetite and weight loss, and isolation from the few friends she did have.

When one lives with a family member who suffers from mental illness, one can become ill without the presence and support of others

When approached by loving family and friends, Janice denied that there was anything wrong, and maintained her orderly routine existence. She continued to mask her true thoughts and feelings. Finally, she was brought to my office after breaking down at work. Janice was afraid to acknowledge her true thoughts and feelings brought on by enormous caretaking responsibilities without any relief in sight. She had grown weary. Family members stated they wanted to help, but somehow, they believed that Janice was the best one for the job. After all, she was single with no other responsibilities, a statement routinely made by insensitive family members.

To complicate matters, Janice was feeling some level of anxiety because of the fear that she too would become sick like her mother. Unfortunately, failure to acknowledge your own condition may make you sick anyway. During the course of therapy, Janice admitted she was even afraid to admit to God what she was going through because she was ashamed of feeling the way she did about caring for her ailing mother. When caring for an ill loved one, it is perfectly normal to feel tired and exhausted because the load can be quite heavy to bear. Give yourself permission to express your thoughts and feelings and seek help from God as well as family and friends.

In some cases, caregivers may need to seek professional help as did Janice because of the potential to become ill themselves. Support groups can also be beneficial in helping caregivers to be reassured that they are not suffering alone, and gain support from those who are in similar care giving situations.

Spiritual Nuggets

In Matthew 11:28-30, what is Jesus' invitation to His children?

Different Strokes for Different Folks

The New Orleans Mardi Gras is famous for the wide variety of beautiful masks tourists can purchase or receive during the celebration. You can be whoever you want to be behind the mask. So it is with many of us. We wear a variety of masks, thinking no one sees what or who is really underneath.

Wearing a mask may disguise your outward appearance, but it may not prevent what's really on the inside from seeping out...

Gloria Morrow, 2005

The Mask of Righteousness

Many people wear the Mask of Righteousness to hide their inner insecurities, feelings of inferiority, fears, and pain. It appears to be easier for people to point out the faults of others than to deal with their own. Jesus had to pull the Mask of Righteousness right off the faces of the Scribes and Pharisees quite often.

Spiritual Nuggets

- What did Jesus attempt to teach the Scribes and Pharisees in John 8:1-59 after they brought the woman who was caught in an adulterous relationship to Him?
- In Matthew 23:1-12, what does Jesus teach the Pharisees about humility? If you are wearing a Mask of Righteousness, continue reading to verse 39.

Yes, we are to strive for Holiness and Righteousness, yet keeping in mind that ALL have sinned and come short of the glory of God, Romans 3:23. Can I keep it real? I am certain that some well meaning Christian sisters are related to the Pharisees, because they prefer to focus on the brokenness of others while ignoring their own.

The Mask of Humor

Have you ever met people who laugh about everything, even when the joke is not funny? In my clinical work, I sometimes talk to people who share some of the most horrific things while smiling and/or laughing. Laughter does contain special healing properties; however laughter is often used as a cover up for pain.

I love to listen to clean comedians, because I love to laugh. However, I have been drawn to the content of some comedians who routinely use their own misfortune and the misfortune of others as the focus of their jokes. It could be said that they are exhibiting healthy behavior by allowing others to laugh with them. But, I am afraid that sometimes these enterprising artists are simply laughing to deal with their own pain. To the outside world, it appears as if they are healthy and wholesome because they have the ability to laugh at themselves, but it is possible that they are secretly attempting to hide how they really feel on the inside.

Spiritual Nuggets

What was Sarah, the wife of Abraham covering up with her laughter in Genesis 18:1-15?

- How do you think Sarah used humor to hide from her situation?
- What was God's response?
- What mask would you have worn if you were Sarah's age and the Lord said you would bear a child?

The Superwoman Mask

Are you a worker bee? A worker bee is one who volunteers to serve on every committee, attempts to take care of a spouse, children, grandchildren, parents, or holds down a job and has a business on the side. The worker bee just might be wearing the Superwoman Mask which is a sign that she too is emotionally unhealthy.

Furthermore, superwomen rarely feel appreciated, and they tend to complain about what others are not doing, even if they have taken on their heavy load voluntarily. The Superwoman Mask may also serve as a cover up for inner pain and low self-esteem. These women tend to DO because it is too difficult to just BE. Are you too busy to BE?

Spiritual Nuggets

In Luke 10:38-42, you will read a fascinating story about Mary and Martha as they make preparation to serve the Master.

- Who was wearing the Superwoman Mask?
- What do you think her motive was?
- What words of advice did she receive from Jesus?

There are other masks people wear to disguise their inner pain. Have you ever met women who appear to have it all together on the outside? Well I have, and these well put together women are wearing a

Mask of Perfection on the outside, but on the inside, they are broken into pieces. On the other hand, instead of wearing a specific type of mask to hide the pain, people use masking or coping devices, such as over-eating, sex, drinking, drugs, gambling, and excessive shopping. Each of these devices may be indicators of poor health and they represent different forms of self-medicating.

Self-Reflection Moment
What device(s) do you use to deal with your pain and hurt?

Benefits of the Mask

Women may continue to wear a mask because of its perceived benefits. They may believe that the mask can help them to present themselves in a positive light in order to win a high approval rating. Unfortunately, those you are seeking approval from are usually unable to grant approval to you in the first place.

Stop looking for approval ratings from mere mortals; rather seek approval from the one who is qualified to give it

Some women believe that the mask can sufficiently hide their true inner thoughts and feelings. While others wear the mask as a shield to protect themselves from further hurt and pain. These benefits are all understandable, but there are a variety of problems that can occur. First, any inauthentic attempt to present yourself in a positive light will certainly surface at some point. The real you will appear, without your permission. Second, the person who keeps the pain buried on the inside is like a time bomb just waiting to explode. Your brokenness will be exposed, and manifest itself in your behavior. For example, you may exhibit a bad attitude as a survival mechanism to keep people from hurting you again. Third, when you work hard to keep people out of your life, you just might be dooming yourself to a lonely and dark prison that God did not intend for you to dwell in.

Consequences of the Mask

There are a variety of consequences associated with wearing a mask to disguise your condition. Failure to take off the mask may result in poor mental, physical, and spiritual health, and the potential for sickness and disease may be much greater. However, the most significant consequence is the impact of the mask on one's Christian witness. Those who continue to mask their pain and brokenness can exhibit inappropriate behaviors that may call into question their level of commitment to God and their Spiritual walk.

For example, Theresa served on the Evangelism team of her church. On the outside, she was a shining example of Christ from head to toe. But on the inside, she was broken and in distress. Theresa wore a

Mask of Righteousness, and each time she went out with the Evangelism team to witness, she was unsuccessful.

Finally, Theresa asked her ministry leader why others were successful in winning souls to Christ and she was not. Thankfully, the ministry leader was honest with her and explained that her attitude was one of self-righteousness, and it was a turn off to those she attempted to minister to. Broken people sometimes put others down by becoming judgmental and self-righteous in their attempt to build themselves up. Further, it was difficult for Theresa to share her personal testimony, which can sometimes be the most powerful closing argument in the gospel presentation.

We must become more transparent if we are going to be a successful witness. Christ calls us to meet people where they are, in their sick condition, as He modeled for us. However, this mandate is impossible without our ability to keep it real and to share our testimony so that others will believe that they too can recover from whatever is ailing them. Everyone at one time or another has a difficult time understanding why they have to suffer. Remember, there is purpose in your suffering, and you and I are called to serve as a living witness of God's goodness and grace.

What's Hiding Underneath the Mask?

A few years ago, my husband took me to the theatre to see the Phantom of the Opera, the famed Broadway musical. The Phantom wore a mask, and I found myself intrigued with what he was covering up on the inside. I was curious about what his face actually looked like. I believe that when you and I uncover ourselves on our journey toward good health, we may find warts of fear, guilt, anger, sadness, low self-esteem, doubt, greed, jealousy, envy, insecurity, hatred, and unforgiveness. Continuing to cover up these warts will certainly lead to poor mental, physical, and spiritual health. Furthermore, if untreated, the warts will be exposed without your consent.

Self-Reflection Moment

Do you know what's hiding underneath your mask?

Who Cares Anyway?

You may be asking yourself this question, who cares anyway? There was a time in my life that I thought no one cared about my silent suffering. I could not receive God's love because I felt unworthy of it. But God has been patient with me, and through His unconditional love, I know beyond a shadow of a doubt that He cares about me, and He cares about you too. God is acquainted with your grief and He wants to minister to your every need.

When we are broken on the inside, it can be very difficult to believe that somebody really cares. That is why we wear the mask in the first place. We tend to guard our hearts from further pain by wearing a mask of protection. But GOD CARES and HE KNOWS.

Critical Dialogues

He Really Knows You

In Psalms 139:1-2, David acknowledges God's sovereignty. God knows everything about you, including your thoughts, feelings, and behaviors. Therefore, any attempt to hide your circumstances and trials from Him is unnecessary. Furthermore, when God places anointed people in your life, they are also able to feel and see beyond your mask because He has appointed them to minister specifically to you.

God also understands you and me better than anyone else. Since Jesus and God are ONE, the dialogue between Jesus and the Samaritan woman at the well in John 4:7-18 supports this notion. When Jesus asked the woman to give Him something to drink, He knew exactly what she was thinking and understood why she had those thoughts. She responded to His request by stating in verse 9, *"how is it that You being a Jew, ask for a drink from me, a Samaritan woman? For Jews have no dealings with Samaritans."*

Jesus knew that the woman was not spiritually equipped to understand why He requested water from her, but He certainly understood why she went there as demonstrated by His response to her: *"If you knew the gift of God, and who it is who says to you, 'Give Me a drink,' you would have asked Him, and He would have given you living water."* Jesus wanted the woman to know that He knew and understood her from the inside out. More importantly, He wanted to teach her that the only way to have all her needs met was by developing a real relationship with Him, the giver of life.

Even though you may be struggling on the inside, Jesus knows and understands. But, He wants you to know Him and trust Him to guide you through every situation. Further, He is aware of why you and I make the decisions we make, and even when we make bad decisions He still loves us and cares about us anyway. He is trying to teach us to get to know and trust Him to avoid continuing to go in the wrong direction. Remember, insanity is doing the same thing the same way, expecting a different result.

He Knows *Where you Are and Where You've Been*

I remember the times in my life when I thought I could hide my stuff from God. But, I like many of you, was inaccurate in my thinking, because God is omnipresent (every place at the same time). I once heard a story about a young girl who was being disobedient to her mother. Her mother warned her by stating: *"Don't you know God is watching you?"* The young girl responded, *"That is impossible Mom. God couldn't be watching me, because I heard the neighbor tell her daughter that God was watching her. You see, God cannot watch us both at the same time."*

We sometimes erroneously believe that God has his eyes on somebody else, therefore, we can continue to hide, or do things that would make God weep if He saw us. But it is critical for Christian women to know that regardless to what we do in secret or what is being done to us in secret, God still loves us and wants to protect, restore, and comfort us.

In John 4:7-18, Jesus demonstrates his ability to know and understand not only our thoughts, but our condition. Sometimes we remain in a state of denial because we are afraid to acknowledge our pain, even to ourselves. So we go through life pretending that it is well with our soul, even though we are defeated and broken on the inside.

The Samaritan woman in the text was in a similar predicament. The Master gave her the opportunity to take the mask off on her own, but she was unable to comply. But Jesus already knew where she was and where she had been, and through His powerful omnipresence, love, and compassion, He changed her life forever. Through the Master's touch, she began to worship Him, and the power of her worship caused the mask to come off on its own. It is impossible for us to worship in spirit and in truth while being held hostage by the mighty grips of hidden pain and suffering.

He Really Loves you

In John 11:33-35, we are reminded that Jesus had feelings too, and He wept. There is some debate from theologians as to why He wept. Some say that Jesus wept because of Mary and Martha's unbelief; while others believe that He wept because He empathized with their pain and had compassion toward them. I believe that Jesus weeps when we offend him, fail to obey His word or doubt Him, and I also believe He weeps when we weep. In fact, Jesus encourages us to weep with those who weep and rejoice with those who rejoice. Jesus weeps with us because He loves us so much. Did you know the father prayed for you and me before we were even conceived in our mother's womb? Please read John 17:20-26 for further confirmation of Jesus' love for His children.

Self-Reflection Moment

After learning in the Scripture that Jesus weeps with those He loves, prayed for you before you were born, died so that you might live, and rose again, how does that make you feel on the inside?

Ready to Remove the Mask?

Are you ready to take the mask off, even if it hurts? If so, you must first develop a willingness to be exposed. I don't know about you, but it was difficult for me to take the mask off initially. Some may call it pride, but I call it fear. I was fearful about how I would go through life without it. After all, I had worn the mask most of my life.

When the mask comes off, you will be left exposed to the elements. Your safety net may appear to be gone. But that safety net is only temporary anyway, and your REAL source of safety is waiting for you to let HIM take control of YOU and YOUR LIFE.

Ouch! That Hurts

Please understand that taking off the mask may inflict pain because it may have been worn so long until it is now very difficult to remove. Have you ever received a facial, and the mask treatment was left on your face too long? I have, and upon its removal, my face began to burn and itch, and a skin rash followed shortly thereafter. So it is with the symbolic masks we wear. Everyone masks pain at one time or another for self-protection, but when we keep the mask on too long, severe damage occurs. Even though it may hurt initially, removing the mask will bring relief if you use the right ingredients.

First, wash your face with a cleansing agent called *honesty*. Be honest with yourself about your condition. When facing your pain you render the enemy powerless. When you are honest with yourself, it may have a stinging effect initially, but feelings of relief will soon occur.

Second, use a good scrub called *prayer*. Prayer will go deep beneath the surface and produce an inner glow and peace that will be apparent on the outside. Prayer removes any blemishes, pimples, or blotches that are seen and unseen by the naked eye.

Third, follow up with an amazing toner called *praise and worship*. Praise and worship is the equalizer because when we offer up praise and worship, we enter into a place with God where we can be totally transparent and vulnerable, yet with inner peace and spiritual strength.

Finally, an excellent moisturizing system called the *whole armor of God* is necessary to protect you from the outside elements, and to help you stand against the enemy. Don't you know you are engaged in spiritual warfare?

Spiritual Nuggets

What does the Word teach us about spiritual warfare in
Ephesians 6:10-19?

Self-Reflection Moment

Engage in honest self-reflection and respond to the following questions:

- Are you wearing a mask today? If so, what type of mask are you wearing?

- What purpose does your mask serve?

- Please identify what is underneath your mask?

- What are you willing to do to begin to remove the mask?

Keeping it Real Testimony!

I had been wearing a mask so long that when I did take the mask off, it hurt really badly. But thank God, the healing did begin. E.H

A Promise from the Master

Jesus said, Come to me all you who labor and are heavy laden, and I will give you rest. Take my yoke upon you and learn from Me, for I am gentle and lowly in heart, and you shall find rest for your souls. For My yoke is easy and My burden is light. Matthew 11:28-30

Chapter Two

Facing the Ghosts of Past and Present

Yea, though I walk through the valley of the shadow of death,

I will fear no evil; for You are with me;

Your rod and staff, they comfort me.

Psalms 23:4 NKJV

In my work as a clinical psychologist, when attempting to make an appropriate diagnosis, I ask clients this question: Do you hear voices? Those suffering from a thought disorder like schizophrenia or those suffering from a depressive disorder, such as bipolar disorder sometimes respond in the affirmative. We call these voices psychotic, and they are unhealthy and potentially harmful to the individual as well as family and friends without appropriate treatment and medication.

But the truth of the matter is we all hear voices, both positive and negative from a variety of sources. My parents are alive and well, and I am still blessed to hear their positive affirmations and encouragement from the past and present in my ears. God also speaks to me, and even when the message does not relay good news, the outcome is always positive. God may give us a warning that danger is looming ahead, or He may give bad news that helps to prepare us for the inevitable. But God also speaks to bring His children closer to Him, and to provide instruction and guidance on how to live the good life and endure to the end.

Spiritual Nuggets

- What did God say to Moses in Exodus 3; and what did you learn about the voice of God in that electrifying passage?
- It is our responsibility to hear His voice and obey. In John 10:1-18, what did you learn about the Good Shepherd?
- God's voice and presence ultimately calls us to a place of repentance and change. How did God's voice change Saul's life forever in Acts 9:3-11?

What is Ghost Talk?

Wouldn't life be just wonderful if we listened to and obeyed the voice of God more often? Unfortunately, we are sometimes unable to hear His voice because it is drowned out by those negative voices we allow to occupy our mental space. I call it *ghost talk,* which refers to the negative voices of past and present that have held you and me hostage for far too long. Your ghost may be a mother, father, stepparent, or spouse, and failure to release the ghost will certainly lead to destruction.

Note: Some of these individuals are important to you, and they cannot be released from your life. They need you and you need them. However, you can release the negative things they have said and done that continue to destroy your life.

I am sometimes haunted by the voices of some of my elementary school classmates who teased me, contributing to my development of poor self-esteem and self-image. There was nothing I could do to stop them from saying mean things, but I did have control over what I allowed myself to believe. But it was too difficult to exercise that level of control as a child, which made me believe every negative word that was spoken. Therefore, environmental factors can be very damaging to the self-esteem of children.

Parents also contribute to their children's development of poor self-esteem and self-concept by name calling, hurtful words, and harsh discipline. Be very careful about the things you say and do to your children because when they are called out of their name and are constantly criticized and abused, they begin to see themselves in a negative light. We must guard our children against ALL negative forces. Remember, the power of life and death is in the tongue.

When Jesus spoke about *unclean spirits* in Mark 9:14-29, He was referring to negative and evil forces that haunted the young man and refused to let him go. Some of you reading this book are haunted by ghosts from the past and present that are not of God, and they are preventing you from living a Godly and healthy lifestyle.

> ### *Self-Reflection Moment*
> How long have you allowed the ghost of past and present
> to reside with you?

The ghost may have shown up without your invitation or your permission to haunt you with negative messages, such as, *you are no good, you are lazy, ugly, dumb*, and the list could go on. The ghosts in your life may have tried to convince you that you are unlovable, and unworthy of being loved. Sadly, we believe the ghosts too easily and tend to live out a self-fulfilling prophesy (confirming other's negative stereotypes and perceptions of you) which paralyzes and prevents us from living life to the fullest. So, we carry the ghosts around with us everywhere we go, making it difficult to hear the voice of God or other positive voices. We seem to be bombarded and overtaken by the presence of negative forces. These forces not only affect your thinking, they also affect your behavior.

However, your ghost(s) may have shown up by invitation only. Perhaps you have invited the ghost to dinner, and never asked him or her to leave. Excessive guilt from past mistakes may keep you tied to the ghosts of past and present, which can ultimately destroy you.

Spiritual Nuggets

What happened to Judas as a result of the guilt he bore for betraying Christ in Matthew 27:3-5?

The ghosts we carry around not only contribute to mental and spiritual death, but to physical death as well, so it is time to face the ghosts in your life, which is the second step toward becoming a healthier you. We cannot forget the work of Satan, who is the chief enemy of God. It is the enemy's desire to interfere with God's plan for your life, so he will continually contribute to your distress and demise. But our fascination and preoccupation with being controlled by the flesh make us an easy target for the enemy.

As stated earlier in this Chapter, your ghost may have been a mother, father, husband, child, boss, co-worker, pastor, friend, abuser, rapist, or others. But again, the first on the list is Satan who has the most to gain from your demise. We have watched Satan move throughout history to try and destroy God's people. In fact, many of God's people in the Bible were haunted by ghosts. This confirms that you are not an original, and more importantly, the same strategies that were used to destroy the evil forces that haunted men and women in the Bible, apply to you and me today.

Damage Done by the Ghost

Can I keep it real? I lived a defeated life because I was stalked by the ghosts of past experiences. I was afraid to return to college because the voices told me I was not smart enough. I was reluctant to use my gift of music to glorify God because of the belief that I was not talented enough; and even after consistently being told that people had been blessed by my music ministry, the ghost talk was more convincing.

The Children of Israel also had ghosts of past experiences to deal with and their presence was a continual stumbling block for them. They were oppressed by the Egyptians (Exodus 1:1-22). While captive they suffered many traumatic experiences, such as enslavement, hard labor, and the most heinous of crimes, the mass murder of male children (Exodus1:15-22). God was concerned about the children of Israel and heard their cry, so he sent Moses to work on their behalf (Exodus 3). Moses appealed to Pharaoh on behalf of the Children of Israel to no avail, resulting in various plagues and atrocities to fall on Pharaoh and the Egyptians (Exodus 5:1-23 – 12:1-36).

God used Moses and others so that the Children of Israel could be released from the grips of their oppressor. God blessed them in such an awesome manner. In fact, they even left with more than they came with (Exodus 12:37-51 – 14:1-12). He assisted them and made sure their oppressor could no longer harm them (Exodus 14:13-31).

At first, the Israelites rejoiced over their new found freedom (Exodus 15:1-21). They were living the good life because God continued to supply all their needs (Exodus 15:22-27). But the ghosts of the past were still present. The experiences at the hand of the oppressor continued to torment and haunt the Children of Israel, which then impacted their attitudes, beliefs, and behaviors in negative ways. It would seem that after all God brought them through, the ghost of Pharaoh and his army would be a fleeting thought, if any. But that was not the case.

Spiritual Nuggets

What evidence supports the presence of the ghosts of past and present?

- They developed a complaining spirit (Exodus 16:1-36 – 17:1-7; Numbers 11:4).

- They broke God's laws (Exodus 32:1-6).

- They were disobedient (Leviticus 10:1-5).

- They began to take on the attitudes, beliefs, and behaviors of Pharaoh, their oppressor (Numbers 12:1-13).

- Finally, they lived in fear and doubt even after watching God perform miracle after miracle both with and without the participation of Moses (Numbers 14:1-3).

Sometimes when we experience traumatic events and pain in our lives, we tend to act out because of our brokenness. One would think that deliverance from oppressive conditions would make us feel better, but like the Children of Israel we continue to struggle. It appeared that while the physical chains and shackles had been removed from the wrists and ankles of the Children of Israel, the mental chains remained intact.

They responded similarly to the African slaves who were brought to America against their will. Once freed physically, many continued to hear the voice of their master and/or slave owner, which negatively impacted their lives and the lives of their children, grand-children, and great grand-children for generations to come.

In my clinical practice, many of the clients I see are clearly damaged by the ghosts of past and present. Unfortunately, the voices have negatively impacted the way they view themselves and others, the way they think others view them, and their attitudes, beliefs, and behaviors. I believe the ghost wreaks havoc in four general areas of functioning that are worth discussing: Psychological/Emotional, Physical, Social, and Spiritual.

Psychological/Emotional Damage

Women who are actively haunted by the presence of ghosts in their lives are at high risk of experiencing psychological/emotional damage. Preoccupation with ghost talk can lead to feelings of sadness, fear, anger, distrust, and the development of a victim's mentality. Women who do not feel good about themselves tend to engage in self-defeating and destructive behaviors such as drinking, drugs, overeating, excessive spending and reckless sexual behaviors in order to feel better. Failure to address this area leads to more debilitating psychological disorders such as depression, anxiety, substance abuse, and eating disorders.

However, the victim mentality may be the most enduring and long lasting of the psychological/emotional damage because those who maintain the victim role are forever locked into the past and chained to those who have hurt them. When engaged in the victim role, we tend to blame others for our condition. The victim consistently waits for the perpetrator to make things right which rarely happens. Therefore, the victim remains chained to the wrongdoer forever, and misses the opportunity to make personal changes that can lead to the "victor" mentality.

As stated earlier, the fictional ghost in many cases creates a generational effect, and it may continue to live through you and future generations resulting in a generational curse. In every good ghost movie, the ghost lives through a live and breathing individual, and it can only live with the help of the person whose body it occupies.

Self-Reflection Moment
Is a ghost living in you? If so, why won't you release it and let it go?

Physical Damage

Women who suffer from psychological/emotional damage are also vulnerable to developing physical health challenges and diseases, such as cancer, heart disease, hypertension, and diabetes. There is a connection between one's mind, body, and spirit, and when the mind is unhealthy, the body and spirit will also pay the price.

Social Damage

The Social Damage of the ghost of the past are also pronounced. Women who are broken have a difficult time developing and maintaining healthy interpersonal relationships, resulting in problems at home, on the job, and at church. Low self-esteem and poor self-image interferes with the quality of marital and family relationships, and individuals who are silently suffering experience social isolation and disconnection. Women that are haunted by the voices of ghosts in their lives are extremely at-risk of experiencing poor relationships in every facet of life.

Spiritual Damage

The Spiritual Damage caused by the ghost of past experience is the most severe because disconnection from God makes it impossible for people to receive true inner healing. Those suffering from Spiritual damage are debilitated in the following ways:

- Disconnection from the Spirit of God due to distrust, failure to study God's Word, lack of prayer, limited praise and worship, and anger toward God.
- Inability to serve or to minister effectively due to fear, or problems with relating or interacting with people effectively.
- Spiritual low self-esteem and feelings of unworthiness.

- Unhealthy religiosity due to over-reliance on religion and traditions to guide one's life instead of the nurturance of a healthy spiritual relationship with God and His people.

Self-Reflection Moment

Who or what haunts you, and how has the ghost(s) damaged your life?

The Benefits of Maintaining the Ghosts

After years and years of living with negative thinking and discouragement, we sometimes grow accustomed to the voices. Even though we do not like what we are hearing, we sometimes become comfortable in our pain and distress. Therefore, some of us hold onto the ghosts in our lives with pride, because we have been fooled into believing that things will never get any better. Remember, the enemy's job is to plant a seed of discouragement, because he knows that seed will continue to grow and you will soon quit by removing yourself as a threat to his evil plot.

Others continue to maintain the ghosts in their lives because it serves as a protection device. In my practice, I have seen beautiful and talented women dress as though they are destitute. They refuse to fix themselves up or do anything to make themselves look more presentable. In talking with some of these women, I have discovered that the ghosts of the past have hurt them in words and deeds, and continuing to appear unappealing protects them from being hurt again. The ghost inside them is screaming, **DON'T COME ANY CLOSER!** But sometimes, we maintain the ghosts to prevent ourselves from saying good-bye to someone we love, even though we really need to.

Self-Reflection Moment

Why is it so hard to say good-bye to someone or something who is constantly hurting you?

The Benefits of Confronting and Releasing Your Ghosts

There are several important benefits of confronting and ultimately releasing the ghosts in one's life.

- You will be freed from the grips of bondage and the ghost(s) will no longer have power over you.
- You will live a healthier and more fulfilled life.
- You will have a healthier self-image.
- You will be better able to reach personal, professional, and spiritual goals.
- You will become a better Christian, wife, mother, daughter, sister, friend, and co-worker.

- You will please God and become a more effective witness for the Kingdom.
- The words that come out of your mouth and the deeds you do will be more positive and life giving.

How can I Face the Ghosts of Past and Present?

1. Acknowledge the damage the ghost is doing to you and those around you and have a true willingness to not only face, but to release the ghost(s) in your life.

2. Connect or reconnect to the Spirit of God. In the book of Job, we see Job being tormented by the enemy, but keep in mind, only with God's permission. Job was forced to confront the enemy. We sometimes erroneously believe that Job simply endured the trauma he experienced like a good soldier without questioning or becoming disheartened with God's decision to allow him to suffer. In fact, Job was a mess, listening to the wrong advice, having suicidal thoughts, and living in total despair because of his tragic situation. When he finally began to understand that God was in control and his source of strength, he was able to submit to the Will of God and he found peace. At that point, the devil no longer held Job hostage. He was set free.

3.   Practice the Spiritual disciplines

> i. Prayer – Ephesians 6:18; Acts 1:12-13; Phil 4:6; I Thess 5:17; 3 John 2
>
> ii. Fasting – Matthew 17:14-21; I Cor. 7:5
>
> iii. Praise – Psalms 146-150
>
> iv. Worship – Psalms 95; John 4:23

4.   Increase your faith – Matthews 8:5-13; Mark 9:24

5.   Speak to yourself in Psalms and Hymns – Ephesians 5:19

6.   Study the Word – II Timothy 2:15

7.   Forgive – Romans 12:19-21; Matthews 5:32; 6:14-15 (For those who may have a problem with forgiveness because it may appear you are excusing the person's bad behavior, read Psalms 94).

8.   Be controlled by the Spirit & not by the flesh – Romans 7 & 8

9.   Call them out and release them – Mark 9:14-29

10.   Speak to a trained professional for Biblically based counseling – Proverbs 11:14.

Spiritual Nuggets

What steps did Jesus take when He got rid of the unclean spirits in the young man in Mark 9:14-29?

Keeping it Real Testimony!

The physical and mental act of burying the ghosts was freeing. Unveiling other ghosts will continue to make me a better person. S.W.

Personal Commitment

Take this time to speak to God about the negative voices that are haunting you. He knows how difficult it is for you, but He wants you to be free. Remember, you may not be able to get rid of people, such as spouses, parents, children, and other family members, but you can prevent their negative words and deeds from destroying you by following the above mentioned steps. If you are ready to confront the ghosts of past and present, please write down all of the negative statements the ghosts have said to you. Tear up that piece of paper into little pieces. Now bury them into the dirt as a symbolic gesture of your willingness to bury the past, so you can be healed and walk toward the future.

Brethren, I do not count myself to have apprehended; but one thing I do, forgetting those things which are behind and reaching forward to those things which are ahead, I press toward the goal for the prize of the upward call of God in Christ Jesus. Philippians 3:13-14 NKJV

Chapter Three

Unpack and Repack the Suitcase

Therefore, we also, since we are surrounded by so great a cloud of witnesses, let us lay aside every weight, and the sin which so easily ensnares us, and let us run with endurance the race that is set before us, looking unto Jesus, the author and finisher of our faith, who for the joy that was set before Him enduring the cross, despising the shame, and has sat down at the right hand of the throne of God. Hebrews 12: 1-2 NKJV

When I was going through my process of healing, which by the way will continue until I leave this earth, I was forced to do something about the heavy suitcases I carried around everyday. Can I keep it real? Once again, I am not alone, because many of you walk around carrying heavy baggage that has resulted in serious injury to your mind, body, and spirit. Let me see if I can paint a clearer picture for you.

A few months ago, I went to the airport to take a flight to Dallas, Texas. I was going to be gone for two weeks, and I was traveling alone. Normally, my husband accompanies me on speaking engagements, but this time he was unable to go. When my husband and I travel together, we usually pack more liberally, because we are allowed to take more pieces of luggage on the plane. However, this time, I had to pack everything for a two week stay in two pieces of luggage. It was my intention to PACK LIGHT, but ladies, you know that is almost impossible for some of us, and the situation was the same for me.

Nonetheless, I took a large suitcase and its smaller companion, and packed everything tightly so it would fit. When I was dropped off at the airport, I could tell that I was going to have a bit of a struggle getting the larger bag checked without paying additional money. While the money was not an issue, who wants to spend extra money for excess baggage when it can be used at the mall? Let me keep it real! I need to stop long enough to point out that carrying around a heavy suitcase will cost you more than you are willing or want to pay.

Well the ticket agent took one look at my bags and said to me in a very polite voice, "I'm sorry miss, but your luggage appears too heavy even without weighing it." I looked straight into the agent's eyes and said, "Why don't you weigh it and we can go from there." There is nothing like positive thinking and faith, but unfortunately, it was what it was, the baggage was clearly over the weight limit.

The kind agent moved a little closer to me and suggested that I take the baggage over to the seating area, and attempt to unpack and repack the two pieces of luggage, and perhaps I would not exceed the limit for either piece. I thought that was a good idea, and after careful unpacking and repacking, the mission was accomplished. I did not have to pay! I am sharing this story with you to demonstrate the importance of carrying a balanced load, because the heavy load you may be carrying is too heavy, preventing you from moving forward. Although difficult, unpacking and repacking your suitcase is a necessary step toward your health and healing.

What was in my Suitcase?

There were four major items in my suitcase that made it very heavy and difficult to carry. The first item was Guilt. I felt guilty because of some of the mistakes I made in my youth. I was unable to forgive myself for those mistakes, and I was covered in guilt. I took total responsibility for my actions, but I forgot to forgive myself.

Women of God, so many of us are plagued by feelings of guilt for mistakes we made in the past. I love to ask people two important questions: How old were you when you made the mistake? If you knew then what you know now would you have made the same mistake? Without fail, the answer is always a resounding NO! When you fully understand that there was purpose in your suffering, you will be able to take guilt out of your suitcase and give God the glory for allowing you to make it through that rough time in your life.

Spiritual Nuggets

Can you see any relief from guilt in Psalms 19:12-14?

The second heavy item in my suitcase was Depression. The guilt made it impossible for me to have joy, so I sunk into a sea of depression. We will discuss depression in Chapter Four, and its debilitating effect on one's life. If you are suffering from depression, you may not even have enough energy to pick your suitcases up, let alone move through the terminal of life. In my situation, the depression knocked me down, and caused me to lose my will to live. Therefore, it is very important to forgive yourself when you mess up.

Spiritual Nuggets

In James 1:2, what does James teach us to do when we make mistakes?

The third item in my suitcase was Anxiety, or fear as it is affectionately called. I was anxious about stepping out on faith and pursuing my purpose on earth because of the ghosts from the past we discussed in Chapter Two. I allowed fear to virtually paralyze me, and I found myself settling for crumbs, when God had a full course meal reserved with my name on it.

> ## *Spiritual Nuggets*
>
> *For God has not given us the spirit of fear; but of power, and of love, and of a sound mind. II Timothy 1:7*

The last heavy item was Anger. I was angry with so many people, including myself until I was consumed with it. In psychology we believe that depression is anger turned inward, and that is exactly how I felt. Because I was a people pleaser, my mask did not reveal how I really felt on the inside. I could feel the anger bubbling inside my body, so rather than expressing it outwardly, I allowed anger to fester on the inside, which created more intense feelings of sadness and anxiety for me.

I did not know how to properly express the anger, and many of you, my sisters, have the same problem. When I did express it outwardly, I would really blow up. Sometimes ladies exhibit passive-aggressive personality traits because they are passive people pleasers as often as possible. But when they blow up, they really become aggressive. Then some of us just have a bad temper, and we blow without much provocation.

Sarah had anger in her suitcase. She became angry after asking Hagar to lay with her husband Abraham to conceive a child. I believe that

Sarah was really angry with herself for allowing her emotions to cause her to make such a foolish decision. She may have also been angry with Abraham for agreeing to the plot. Nonetheless, Sarah's anger was expressed in an inappropriate manner (Genesis 16:6).

God wants us to express our anger (which is a normal emotion) in an appropriate and Godly manner. Failure to do so usually results in disaster. We sometimes fail to express anger in an appropriate way to the intended target; therefore, innocent bystanders often get caught in the cross-fire.

Spiritual Nuggets

How does God instruct us to deal with anger in

James 1:19-20 and Ephesians 4:26?

What's in your Suitcase?

Can I keep it real? I am not the only woman who has heavy items in her suitcase. You've got some heavy items in your suitcase too. Perhaps it would be useful for you to identify what you have packed in your suitcase, such as fear, anger, hatred, unforgiveness, jealousy, envy, pride that may be weighing you down, preventing you from living a healthy and purpose driven life.

Self-Reflection Moment

Take a few moments to answer the following questions:

- What's in your suitcase?

- How did it get there?

- Why is it so difficult to unpack?

Consequences of Dead Weight

After my husband dropped me off at the airport, I was forced to attempt to handle my own bags once the agent suggested that I unpack and repack them. The weight of the bags began to put strain on my forearms, and I began to feel the pain. So it is with the heavy suitcases we carry around. They begin to feel like dead weight, causing us to experience mental, physical, and spiritual pain and anguish.

The heavy weight of the suitcase also impacts our decision making. Reflecting back on my early experiences, I can clearly see how carrying around an over stuffed suitcase caused me to make unhealthy decisions. Can I keep it real? Even now, every once I awhile, I still make decisions out of my unhealthy place. However, I have been successful in holding myself accountable with the help of God, so that those occasions are less frequent. I can almost guarantee that your heavy suitcases have also contributed to some of the unhealthy decisions you have made and those you continue to make.

Spiritual Nuggets

Read Genesis 19 to gain a clearer understanding of the negative consequences of dead weight. You will find that Lot's wife was certainly overloaded because of a series of important events.

- Evil infiltrated their community – Genesis 19:1-7.
- Lot was not a strong Spiritual leader and he offered his daughters to be raped and pillaged by evil men in the community – Genesis 19:8-11.
- A death sentence had been declared on Sodom forcing the family to relocate and leave everything behind – Genesis 19:12-16.
- The city was destroyed – Genesis 19:24-25.
- It is possible that Lot's wife was carrying heavy dead weight that was difficult to unload, such as: depression, anxiety, fear, shame, guilt, anger, and greed.
- Lot's wife failed to unload the excess baggage preventing her from moving forward, and eventually causing her demise – Genesis 19:26.

How can I unpack and repack my suitcase?

- Continue to develop and mature spiritually through prayer and meditation, fasting, daily devotional, and praise and worship.

- Give yourself permission to take the dead weight out of your suitcases. Read Hebrews 12:1-3.

- Consider repacking your suitcase with the fruit of the Spirit found in Galatians 5:17-26 to achieve balance and to lighten your load.

- Forgive yourself and those who have hurt you.

- You may need some help in unpacking and repacking the suitcase, so do not be ashamed to seek the help of a trained Christian counselor to help you through this process.

Self-Reflection Moment

After prayer, go through your suitcase and make a decision about at least one item that you are willing to unpack. After reading Galatians 5:17-26 write down the item(s) you are willing to put into the suitcase to achieve a Spiritual balance. Put this personal commitment in a place where you can retrieve it when you need it the most.

Keeping it Real Testimony!

The week we unpacked and repacked our suitcases, I really wanted to get rid of some of the "stuff" I had been carrying around, and I did. I repacked patience in my suitcase and I have sincerely made an effort to practice this in my relationships with family, peers, and especially my students. P.W.

The Lord upholdeth all that fall, and raiseth up all those that be bowed down. The eyes of all wait upon thee; And thou givest them their meat in due season. Psalms 145:14-15

Chapter Four

Abandon the Never Ending SAGA

I called on the Lord in distress; The Lord answered me and set me in a
broad place. The Lord is on my side; I will not fear.
What can man do to me? Psalms 118:5-6

Judy, a 25-year old woman came to my office after being referred by her employer. She was having a difficult time controlling her anger, and she was also becoming increasingly sad and anxious. Judy probably had good reason to feel as she did. At the age of 7, Judy was sexually molested repeatedly until the age of 11 by a male family member. The abuse was never reported because the perpetrator told Judy her mother would be very angry if she discovered what happened. He assured her it was really her fault because of the way she sat on his lap. Judy believed him and kept quiet about her traumatic ordeal which only stopped because the perpetrator was killed in an automobile accident on his 23rd birthday.

Judy buried their secret in the grave with him, and remained silent, although traumatized.

Judy had suffered an emotional trauma that had the potential to impact the rest of her life in negative ways. Regardless of its source, an emotional trauma contains three common elements:

- it was unexpected
- the person was unprepared
- there was nothing the person could have done to prevent it from happening

When Judy reached her 13th birthday, she began to act out sexually, and lived a life of promiscuity throughout her teen and early adult years. She became pregnant when she was 16, but terminated the pregnancy without her mother's knowledge. She became pregnant again when she was 18, but decided to keep the baby. She carried this baby to term, but the baby was still born. Judy was devastated and her saga continued with news from her gynecologist that she may never be able to have another child for health reasons.

Judy had a poor relationship with her mother since she was an adolescent, and her father was absent. She was also an only child, with a very limited social support system. Judy's mother had recently become a Christian, and Judy attended church services with her on special occasions, but she was still angry with God and everyone else. Everything began to unravel, and Judy's anger began to consume her life. She was also very fearful of men, even though she was sexually active. When any man of substance attempted to get close to her, Judy could not handle it and would find some way to sabotage the relationship. She was afraid.

When girls experience molestation at a young age, they are very much at-risk of experiencing some of the signs and symptoms of PTSD (Post Traumatic Stress Disorder which will be discussed later in this Chapter). Judy recalled experiencing flash backs of the perpetrator coming into her room when her mother was sleep, and these visual images persisted into adulthood.

Judy also had very poor interpersonal skills, and was argumentative. She would blow up over very small things, and finally her anger contributed to her being put on administrative leave. Judy was mandated to attend anger management classes and individual therapy. Judy's mental/emotional health was very poor, because of traumatic experiences she endured in silence as a child.

During my initial assessment of Judy, it was apparent that she was suffering from what I have termed as the SAGA Syndrome, which is an acronym for Sadness, Anxiety, Guilt, and Anger. When individuals suffer from this syndrome, they ultimately suffer from a Broken Spirit. For example, depression can occur because of guilt, and result in anger and anxiety. Likewise, the guilty person tends to be angry, sad, and anxious.

THE SAGA SYNDROME

Those who suffer from the SAGA Syndrome inevitably develop poor mental health. Therefore, I believe it is very important for women to abandon the SAGA syndrome in order to lead a healthier life.

What Constitutes Poor Mental Health?

People who are mentally unhealthy tend to experience difficulty in making everyday decisions, have difficulty setting and reaching goals, exhibit inappropriate behavior, display negativity, experience emotional highs and lows on a regular basis, and their daily functioning is impaired.

How Did I get Here?

Early Beginnings

When children do not experience a healthy childhood because of early separation and relocation from family of origin due to abuse or other traumatic events, it is very likely that those children will develop poor mental health if early effective interventions are not implemented.

Believing the Hype

When the voices of past and present tell you that *you won't make it, or you will never be anything,* you have the strong potential to believe those voices. This thinking along with your own negative self-talk, such as *it's all my fault, I'm incompetent, and I can't,* also contribute to the development of poor mental health.

Spiritual Disconnection

Spiritual disconnection may be the most problematic of all, because failure to remain connected to God will surely make you sick.

Failure to turn to the Lord leads to disaster that can make one lose one's mind. Too many of us are struggling in this area because either we have never really accepted Jesus Christ as Lord and Savior, or we are spiritually immature, because we have failed to develop a healthy relationship with the Lord.

WE ARE ALL BROKEN

What does it mean to be broken? Not complete or free, violently separated into parts, shattered, damaged, fractured, irregular, made weak, interrupted, crushed, bankrupt, cut-off, disconnected. We are all broken to one degree or another. Some may be cracked while others are shattered. Keep in mind however, that if you are broken, you may be just where God wants you to be. Sometimes, He has to break us in order to make us over again.

Spiritual Nuggets

What does Psalms 51:17 teach us about brokenness?

Nonetheless, some have a real difficult time dealing with their pain and suffering brought on by life's challenges and traumatic events, which can contribute to the development of mental illnesses such as depression, anxiety, post-traumatic stress disorders, and other psychological problems.

Impact of Emotional Trauma

The song writer said it like this: *Life is filled with swift transitions."* Tragedy and crises will come, sometimes with a vengeance. When you and I are emotionally and spiritually healthy, we are better equipped to handle life's challenges, crises, and calamities. Can I keep it real? Even though you may feel grounded in the Word and have a close relationship with God, you too can become shattered when hit by a major challenge of life. Therefore, it is very likely that those who are not connected to God, are more at-risk of suffering from psychological impairment as the result of a severe emotional trauma.

I had the privilege of serving time in Dallas, Texas after Hurricane Katrina to assist the survivors in meeting their psychological needs. It is safe to say that no one was exempt from being traumatized by that horrific disaster because of the significant loss of life, property, shelter, and familiar surroundings. Even those who watched in horror all over the world experienced some level of trauma.

But those who already suffered from psychological distress (both treated and untreated) may have been impacted more significantly. I also suspect that those with no connection with God were even more debilitated in the aftermath of Hurricane Katrina. Therefore, it is highly possible that some of the survivors were and still are particularly at-risk of developing psychological disorders, such as PTSD after experiencing an emotional trauma of this magnitude.

What is Depression?

Depression is a treatable disease, with the following signs and symptoms:

- Persistent sad, anxious or "empty" mood
- Feelings of hopelessness, pessimism
- Feelings of guilt, worthlessness, helplessness
- Loss of interest or pleasure in hobbies and activities that were once enjoyed, including sex
- Decreased energy, fatigue
- Difficulty concentrating, remembering and making decisions
- Insomnia, early-morning awakening, or oversleeping
- Appetite and/or weight loss or overeating and weight gain
- Restlessness, irritability
- Persistent physical symptoms that do not respond to treatment, such as headaches, digestive disorders, and chronic pain
- Thoughts of death or suicide, suicide attempts

(Source: National Institute of Mental Health)

Failure to treat depression can sometimes lead to suicidal thoughts and behaviors, even when one knows and loves God!

Warning Signs of Suicide

Published By
Hope Allianz, Inc. Counseling and Healing Center

- The individual has attempted suicide before.
- A family member has successfully committed suicide.
- The individual has had a recent severe loss or losses.
- The individual loses interest in their personal appearance.
- The individual is talking or joking about suicide (e.g., committing suicide themselves or talking about it in general.
- The individual is preoccupied with death and dying (e.g., recurrent death themes in music, literature, drawings, writing letters or leaving notes referring to death or "the end."
- The individual is making statements about being reunited with deceased loved one.
- The individual has trouble eating and sleeping.
- The individual experiences drastic changes in their behavior.
- The individual withdraws and isolates from family, friends, or social activities.
- The individual loses interest in things they care about (e.g., hobbies, work, and school).
- The individual prepares for death by making out a will and making final arrangements as if to set one's affairs in order.
- The individual gives away personal possessions.
- The individual is making statements about hopelessness, helplessness, or worthlessness (for example, "life is useless." "Everyone would be better off without me." "It does not matter, I won't be around anyway." "I wish I could just disappear."
- The individual becomes suddenly happier and calmer.
- The individual makes unusual visits or calls to people they care about..saying their goodbyes.
- The individual participates in self-destructive behaviors (e.g., alcohol or drug abuse, self-injury or manipulation, promiscuity).
- The individual participates in risk-taking behaviors (e.g., reckless driving, or excessive speeding, carelessness around bridges, cliffs or balconies, or walking in front of traffic).
- The individual talks about going home to be with the Lord.

**National Suicide Hotline
1-800- SUICIDE**

What is Anxiety?

Anxiety is a normal reaction to stress. It helps one deal with a tense situation in the office, study harder for an exam, and remain focused on an important speech. In general, it helps one cope. But when anxiety becomes an excessive, irrational dread of everyday situations, it has become a disabling disorder. Common types of anxiety include: fearfulness, worry, dread, panic, obsession, compulsion.

Symptoms of Anxiety

Anxiety produces **physical** symptoms such as:

- rapid or irregular heartbeat (palpitations)
- stomach problems (gnawing feeling, nausea, "butterflies," diarrhea, irritated bowel syndrome)
- breaking out in a sweat, or feeling cold and clammy
- headaches, lightheadedness or dizziness
- body tension or aches
- fatigue or feeling out-of-breath
- shaking, trembling or twitching
- difficulty falling asleep or staying asleep

Emotional symptoms of anxiety include:

- a general sense of apprehension and dread
- nervousness

- jumpiness
- irritation
- fearfulness
- isolation from others
- feeling incredibly self-conscious and insecure

Spiritual Nuggets

The Scripture teaches us to be anxious for nothing! Phil 4:6

What is Post Traumatic Stress Disorder (PTSD)?

PTSD can occur when one is exposed to a traumatic event, such as Hurricane Katrina, or exposure to an ongoing traumatic situation, such as living in an abusive environment. It can trigger severe debilitating emotional reactions characterized by intrusive thoughts, painful physical symptoms and a lingering sense of dread. PTSD can be exacerbated by early life trauma that includes isolation as well as abuse. Abuse or violence suffered over a long period of time can lead to the development of psychological disorders, such as depression and anxiety. Also, poverty can have a similar effect, particularly where there is an absence of a secure and supportive home environment.

In the case of Judy, she reported having suicidal thoughts with at least two prior attempts to take her own life. Feelings of sadness and anxiety were the result of the abuse and other family issues surrounding the fact that she did not have a good relationship with her mother and absent father. She was dealing with insurmountable guilt by holding herself totally responsible for the traumatic events, the promiscuous lifestyle, the abortion, the loss of her baby, and the inability to have a child. The guilt was almost unbearable, and the anger became even more intensified.

The SAGA Syndrome can prevent one from fulfilling one's purpose on earth. These emotional barriers can easily lead to more serious mental and physical health problems. Therefore, Judy's failure to be connected to God and to seek professional help earlier may have contributed to her current condition. Most of the serious mental health disorders occur because early signs and symptoms of distress go untreated. The SAGA Syndrome can also occur because of the heavy suitcases we carry around and relief is achieved by some sort of clinical intervention by a trained professional, such as talk therapy and sometimes medication with appropriate consultation.

Judy's situation appeared to be exacerbated by the development of a victim's mentality. As stated earlier, when a woman takes on the victim role, it is very difficult for her to heal because she wallows in self-pity while at the same time waiting for the perpetrator or someone to make things right. Judy was waiting for a dead man to apologize for the things he did to her. She allowed herself to be haunted by his evil deeds, which then impacted how she viewed herself, other family members, and the world.

The victimization mentality feeds into the SAGA Syndrome, and those of you who are unable to release it will have a more difficult time recovering from the past trauma in your lives. Furthermore, failure to work through your issues impacts your behavior in negative ways. So while you may have been victimized, you have the potential to victimize others.

I remember watching a movie that illustrated this point. A young woman had been abused then rejected and mistreated by several men in her life because of the way she looked. She was unattractive according to the world's standards. After suffering enormous humiliation and pain, she decided to have plastic surgery and upon completing her treatment she looked like a totally different person. She then pursued each of the men who rejected her and eventually murdered them one by one. We may not commit physical murder, but our actions are killing us on the inside and therefore, may be harmful to those around us, even if they were not responsible for our pain.

They Were No Different

We all suffer from some level of brokenness, and Jesus' disciples were no exception. Both Judas and Peter suffered from the SAGA Syndrome. We do not know very much about Judas' personal life, but his behavior demonstrated that he was broken like you and me.

Spiritual Nuggets

- How does Judas exhibit signs of the SAGA Syndrome in John 12:3-6; Matthew 26: 14-25; Matthew 27:3-10?

- How does Peter exhibit signs of the SAGA Syndrome in Matthew 14:28-33; 26:51-53 and 69-75; Mark 8:31-33; 14:66-72; Luke 22:54-65.

Consequences of the SAGA Syndrome

Women who suffer from the SAGA Syndrome are at risk of experiencing poor mental, physical, and spiritual health. However, the SAGA syndrome can be lethal to our connection with God. When we are experiencing mental health challenges, we sometimes have a difficult time focusing on God and going to His sanctuary for comfort. Further, in our despair, we may become angry with God for allowing us to go through pain and suffering. We also get angry and upset when we see those around us prospering, especially if they have done us wrong.

You remember Asaph in Psalms 73. He kept his eye on the wicked and their perceived level of prosperity. He became so angry until he had to take a sabbatical from the church. But when he reached his lowest point, he went back to the sanctuary of God. I believe that the sanctuary did not have to be a church house. Rather, it could have been that quiet place where Asaph would go to commune with God. Once there, he was reminded of the goodness and awesomeness of God. Some of us need to revisit the sanctuary of God so that we can begin to commune with Him once again, and to feel his presence as we go through life's challenges.

What does Sin have to do with it?

The SAGA Syndrome can also occur, however because of sin and failure to walk in obedience to God. I am sure we have good reason for the decisions we make. We can blame our fathers, mothers, husbands, sisters, children everyday of the week, but God still holds us accountable for our actions. Let us look at the various ways we sin in response to the emotional trauma we have experienced.

For those of you who have suffered abuse and molestation, you may attempt to resume power and take control over your lives by acting out sexually. Your behavior is sinful. Your husband may not be meeting your needs, so you withhold your love from him. Guess what, that behavior is also sinful. God has called you out for Christian service, but you refuse. That is another example of sin.

Others of you simply nurture and embrace hatred, anger, and unforgiveness. You know that's sin! I once heard a minister say: *Harboring hatred in your heart is like drinking poison, expecting your enemy to drop dead.* In other words, if you fail to forgive, you shall surely die, and your enemy may live to attend your funeral! Please know that the underlying source of sin is disobedience.

Again, there may be a good reason for your behavior, but God is still holding you accountable to Him, and unfortunately, you will have to face the consequences of your actions.   One could say that David, being short in stature, suffered teasing from his brothers and the other sheep herders, which may have contributed to low self-esteem and possibly the development of the "Little Man's Complex."   One could also say that the "Little Man's Complex," was responsible for his winning warrior status, and the desire to take whatever he wanted, even if it left blood on his hands.   Regardless to the psychological explanation of David's behavior, God still held him accountable and he had to face the consequences of his ungodly response to his inner turmoil.

Spiritual Nuggets

- What were the consequences of David's sin with Bathsheba found in 2 Samuel 12:10-12; 15-19?

- Which elements of the SAGA Syndrome did David exhibit because of his sins?

- What did David ask God to do for him in Psalms 51? He will do the same for you and me.

How can we Abandon the SAGA Syndrome?

In order to abandon the SAGA Syndrome, there are three important areas of response: Psychological, Physical, and Spiritual.

Psychological Response

Sometimes our emotional trauma has gone on so long until we need help from a trained professional who is anointed by God. The faith community has a difficult time embracing the realization that people sometimes require the assistance of trained professionals who are called by God in this area. There are a variety of reasons for the difficulty in this area, however, the most popular reason is the stigma associated with mental illness among the body of Christ.

Many among the body of Christ have been taught that psychological problems are the result of sin and a lack of faith. Those who are suffering from psychological problems may prefer to do so in silence because they do not want to be labeled as weak or sinful. While sin and a lack of faith certainly can contribute to your level of brokenness, it is important to understand that psychological disorders such as depression, anxiety, and PTSD are treatable diseases that may require talk therapy and medication by trained mental health professionals to prevent more severe mental health problems from surfacing.

Christian women must never fail to seek God's help for psychological problems, because He is the master healer. But it is equally important to understand and know that God uses people to help broken people.

Physical Response

I am certain that the emotional trauma you have experienced has also impacted your physical body. Be sure to get a medical workup annually to prevent health issues from invading you. Do not forget to establish a healthy diet, exercise at least three times each week, drink 6-8 glasses of water each day, and get plenty of sunshine and rest. Those of you who are menopausal are highly at risk of experiencing symptoms of depression and anxiety. So get a check-up by your primary care physician.

Spiritual Response

If you are suffering from the SAGA Syndrome, I can almost guarantee that you are in need of a spiritual check-up. Study God's Word and seek to be controlled by the Spirit of God in order to enjoy inner peace and make Godly decisions. Further, increase your faith through prayer and fasting (Matthew 17:20-21), and be obedient by surrounding yourself with Godly people (Philippians 2:12). I realize it is sometimes difficult to pray when you are going through. But Romans 8:26-27 teaches that the Holy Spirit makes intercession on our behalf when we cannot do it ourselves. Forgive yourself and others (Matthew 18:20-35; Romans 12:17-21), and develop a spirit of gratitude. Please keep in mind that your situation could be or could have been worse, so count your blessings, one by one, and thank God for helping you to overcome every situation.

Spiritual Nuggets

How does the Word teach us to handle each situation? Look in your Bible Concordance/Index and find Scriptures to fill in the opposite side.

SADNESS		**JOY**	
1.	Proverbs 12:25	1.	
2.	Nehemiah 2-8	2.	
3.	Ezekiel 13:22-23	3.	
ANXIETY		**FAITH**	
1.	Deuteronomy 31:16	1.	
2.	Psalms 118:5-6	2.	
3.	Proverbs 12:25	3.	
4.	Proverbs 29:25	4.	
5.	Psalms 27	5.	
6.	Philippians 4:6-7	6.	
7.	Luke 12:22-34	7.	
8.	2 Timothy 1:7	8.	
9.	I John 4:18	9.	
10.	Matthews 8:26	10.	
GUILT		**FORGIVENESS**	
1.	Romans 3:21-29	1.	
2.	Romans 4:6-8	2.	
3.	Romans 8:1	3.	
4.	Philippians 3:13-14	4.	
5.	I Timothy 1:12-17	5.	
6.	I John 3:19-20	6.	
ANGER		**PEACE**	
1.	Ecclesiastes 7:9	1.	
2.	Proverbs 15:1	2.	
3.	Proverbs 20:2	3.	
4.	Ephesians 4:26-32	4.	
5.	Proverbs 29:22	5.	
6.	Psalms 37	6.	

Self-Reflection Moment

What personal commitment are you willing to make to begin the process

of abandoning the SAGA Syndrome?

Keeping it Real Testimony!

I have learned that I am my own worse enemy. Once I decided to stop

worrying about things outside my control, I began to feel better, more

calm and more at peace with myself. R.B.

There is therefore now no condemnation to them which are in Christ

Jesus, who walk not after the flesh, but after the Spirit. Romans 8:1

Chapter Five

Accept Your New Father

I will be a Father to you, and you shall be My sons and daughter, says the Lord Almighty. 2 Corinthians 6:18 NKJV

The relationship between daddy and daughter is very important. In fact, it is often the first love relationship for girls. This unique relationship can promote increased feelings of self-esteem and self-worth, and it can prevent girls from falling victim to the voice of the wrong daddy figure. But most importantly, this critical love relationship increases the potential for the development of trust in other males, and even God Himself. Unfortunately, when fathers are not active in their daughter's lives, and they fail to provide love and nurturance, there is the potential for all future relationships to be destroyed. Further, negative and self-destructive behaviors can persist.

Daddy's Little Princess

We most often hear people say how important it is for boys to have fathers in their lives. I agree wholeheartedly. But I believe it is of equal importance for girls to grow up with loving fathers, because there is growing evidence that fathers are also critical to their growth and development into womanhood.

I know firsthand the value of girls having a loving father in their lives because I have a very special relationship with mine. I am the oldest daughter of five siblings. My parents have always loved and cherished all their children to the best of their ability. I think that all of us have a special and unique relationship with each of our parents which have been very important to our sense of self and overall well-being.

My father is a strong Christian man with a serious love for God. He has always made me feel special, like his little princess, even though he loves all his children madly. Unfortunately, I paid more attention to what people outside the home thought of me, but my father gave me a special gift to help me to remember how special I am. He tells this story, and I can recite it verbatim because he has told the same story for as long as I can remember.

In the words of my Dad!

"Gloria is my blessed child. I was getting older and I asked God for a child. I told God if He gave me a child, I would serve Him the rest of my days. Well, God answered my prayers, and after she was born I never touched another drink or smoked another cigarette. I gave my life totally to Christ, and I want everyone to know that Gloria is a blessed child, even today."

I cannot tell you how important that testimony has been to me, especially since I have been an adult. It didn't mean very much to me when I was younger, and I used to feel embarrassed when he said it from the pulpit. But today, it is a great source of pride. His positive, affirming, and nurturing voice and the words he uses to describe his love and adoration for me have given me the proper ammunition to fight against the negative forces we talked about earlier in this book. Let me keep it real!

My father has also been a great example, and he has helped to shape my attitude toward men as well as taught me the important qualities to look for in a man. It is amazing how many of his qualities my husband shares [those that I love and admire, and those I could live without]. Thank God, the positive certainly outweigh the negative. I have truly been blessed for I am my daddy's little princess no matter how old I get.

Where is my Tiara?

Even though I have had a wonderful experience in my relationship with my father, I am painfully aware that many women have not had the same kind of father experience, which unfortunately has negatively impacted their relationship with men and with God. They are still looking for their dads to crown them with their own little Tiara. However, it is difficult for fathers to treat their daughters like a princess, when they have not been taught how to be a king. As women, we sometimes expect our fathers and the men in our lives to treat us like royalty, when in fact; they have not received royal grooming. Men who have been groomed for royalty understand the royal rules of engagement, and they are better equipped to serve comfortably in the role.

When fathers have not had good role models of fatherhood, are broken themselves, and lack a connection with God, they are rarely able to demonstrate the traits and characteristics of a loving father. So if you have become angry with your father because he did not meet your expectations, you may be exerting unnecessary energy for the king does not exist.

Who Killed the King?

Many fathers have every intention on playing an active role in the lives of their children. However, sometimes the king is not allowed to be involved because of separation and divorce, illness, lack of financial resources, and other life circumstances. It is important to understand why your daddy was not the king you wanted him to be, because perhaps his lack of involvement was out of his control. Someone (a wife, mother, or other significant person) may have killed the king before he could even sit on the throne. This is certainly a possibility when parents separate and go through a bitter divorce.

Love Note

Ladies, it is very important to make sure children are encouraged to love and respect both parents. I know you are hurt over the divorce, but when you allow yourself to put the children in the middle of your mess, they will suffer for what seems like an eternity. They want to love you both, even those new step-parents. So don't allow your anger and hurt to cause your children to be cut in half, because the survival rate is not very good.

Spiritual Nuggets

How did the wise mother demonstrate true love for her child in I Kings 3:16-28?

Self-Reflection Moment

- Would you rather see your children cut in half than to give them permission to love and be loved by their father?
- What are some of the consequences of cutting them in half?

You Shall Overcome

I asked a dear friend of mine to share her story to help those of you reading this book without good father relationships to know that you can overcome it with the help of your Heavenly Father. Leslie, a 59 year old marketing executive shared her father story with me. She recalls that her father was in the home, but he was a very quiet man who primarily stayed in his room when he came home from work. Leslie stated, "All I wanted to do was to tell him about my day, and have him read me a story at bedtime. But he was absent even though he was in the home."

Leslie's mother was the dominant figure in the home, and she was physically abusive to Leslie and her younger brother. Most of her life, Leslie blamed her father for not protecting them from their mother. Leslie, having been married multiple times, had never had a successful marriage, and she devoted most of her life to her career. It was very difficult for her to trust a man or to rely on one for support, comfort, and protection and provision. In fact, she had a hard time viewing God as her protector and provider.

Finally, through doing personal work in therapy and attending a Bible teaching church in her community, she was able to accept a new father, one that we know to be our *Jehovah-Jireh* which means ultimate provider. However, she had to forgive her earthly father in order to embrace Jesus, her new one. Through this therapeutic process, Leslie was also able to forgive her mother.

Long after childhood has ended, women can sometimes continue to suffer from the loss of a loving father relationship, which gets in the way of healthy love relationships of all types. Natalie, a 35 year old retail worker finds this statement to be true.

> *"He did not beat me, but he beat my mom. I remember hiding under my bed to escape the loud noises and the sound of my mother screaming and crying as he would beat her unmercifully. I was only 8 years old then. One day, I could not take it any longer, and I bolted from my hiding place, and ran and jumped on my father's back to pull him off my mother. Even though I was a teenager by this time, he was still stronger than me, and he threw me off his back and I went flying into the air, finally landing on the floor. I remember feeling the pain of the fall, but nothing hurt more than seeing my mother accept the flowers and candy he would bring her during the honeymoon stage. She seemed to forget all he did to her and to us"*

Natalie identifies herself as a Christian, but she tends to see God as a punitive father and this thinking has caused her to live an unhealthy and unbalanced Christian life. She is afraid that God will severely punish her for any mistakes she has made, so Natalie hides under the Mask of Self-Righteousness to avoid God's wrath. She is unable to accept God as a loving father because she has never experienced the real love of her earthly father. As for men, even though she does not trust them, she still managed to get into an abusive relationship herself. She remains in an unhealthy marriage because she is more afraid of displeasing God and looking for male acceptance than placing herself in a safer situation.

Women still bear the scars of being separated from their fathers due to separation, divorce, and death. A growing number of girls do not grow up with their fathers because they are incarcerated. Perhaps you are still angry because he left, especially if your mother never recovered from his departure.

A Message to Mothers

I know it is hard when a spouse or significant other decides to end the relationship and leaves. It is even more difficult when a man leaves to begin a new family. But mothers, we must be careful to not allow our anger and hurt to turn to bitterness. If it does, that bitter root will do more damage to you and your children than the intended perpetrator. Find a way to give your children permission to love their father in spite of what happened between the two of you. Make a vow to avoid Baby Mama Drama at all cost because you may actually become the villain instead of the victim in your children's eyes.

Self-Reflection Moment

- What expectations, if any, did you have of your father figure?
- If you could give your father figure a report card in this area, what grade would you give him, and why?
- What promises did your father figure keep and how did this impact your life?
- What promises did your father figure break and how did this impact your life?
- What lessons (both positive and negative) did you learn from your father figure?

When fathers have been absent, or they failed to love and nurture their daughters, these now adult women feel a sense of abandonment and rejection, and they experience a lack of emotional and sometimes financial support. More important, however, these situations then impact their ability to believe and receive God's love; for how could a just God allow a father to behave as the fathers mentioned above? Furthermore, if God is our heavenly Father, isn't it likely that He will behave like our earthly Father? Many women erroneously compare God to their earthly fathers, when the two can never be compared.

Self-Reflection Moment

How does your earthly father compare to your Heavenly Father?

EXAMPLE

Earthly Father	Heavenly Father
A man	A Spirit
Imperfect	perfect
Broken	Whole
Limited	Infinite
Unfaithful	Faithful

- Please feel free to add to the above-mentioned list.
- Can you think of other differences between your earthly father and your Heavenly Father?
- Is it fair to continue to put God in the same category as your earthly father? Why or why not?

Did Your Father Really Know What to Do?

Both parents are critical to their children's overall well-being, and they each are responsible for loving and nurturing the children God has blessed them with. Unfortunately, some fathers may not know their spiritual duty, or the duties they were to perform because of their own spiritual disconnection from God. Perhaps your father was never connected in the first place. Fathers who have a real relationship with God and know and understand His word tend to be better equipped to parent than those who do not. So let us visit the Scripture to gain a better understanding of the duties that both fathers and mothers should perform in the lives of their children.

<table>
<tr><td colspan="2" align="center">***Spiritual Nuggets***</td></tr>
<tr><td>**SCRIPTURE**</td><td>**PARENTAL DUTIES**</td></tr>
<tr><td>Titus 2:4</td><td>_____</td></tr>
<tr><td>Prov 22:6; Eph 6:4; Deut 4:9;11;19; Isaiah 38:19</td><td>_____</td></tr>
<tr><td>Gen 48:15; Heb 11:20</td><td>_____</td></tr>
<tr><td>Job 42:115; 2 Cor 12:14; I Tim 5:8</td><td>_____</td></tr>
<tr><td>Prov 13:24; 19; 23:13; 29:17; Heb 12:7</td><td>_____</td></tr>
<tr><td>Eph 6:4; Col 3:21</td><td>_____</td></tr>
<tr><td>Gen 17:18; I Chr 29:19</td><td>_____</td></tr>
<tr><td>Matt 19:13-14</td><td>_____</td></tr>
</table>

Perhaps this exercise will be helpful in enhancing and improving your parenting skills with your own children.

Self-Reflection Moment

For those of you who have not had a healthy father/daughter relationship, God desires to become your new Father. Guess what, He really wants to become your Father even if you have or had a good earthly father. He knows you have been abandoned, rejected, and oppressed, and He is acquainted with and understands your grief. But He has promised never to leave you nor forsake you. Read Jeremiah 31 to review the promises of God:

- God can give us joy to replace the sorrow.
- God expresses His love for the children of Israel.
- He promises to rebuild them, like He will rebuild you and me.
- He shall provide everything we need.
- He will dry every tear stained eye.
- He will restore you.
- He will have mercy on you.

Remember, He knows what you have been through. In the 28th verse it says, *and it shall come to pass that as I have watched over them to pluck up, to break down, to throw down, to destroy, and to afflict, so I will watch over them to build and to plant, says the Lord.* I know you thought that God was not watching and that He left you too. But He knows and He cares. In verse 9 of the text, He assures us in His word. *They shall come with weeping, and with supplications I will lead them. I will cause them to walk by the rivers of waters, in a straight way in which they shall not stumble. FOR I AM A FATHER TO ISRAEL, and Ephraim is my firstborn.*

LADIES, GOD WANTS TO BE YOUR FATHER TOO!

Spiritual Nuggets

Read Proverbs 4 & 2 Corinthians 6-11-18 for a Father's Advice

---

We allow our disconnection and anger with God and perhaps our own fathers to pave the way for us to link up with ungodly people to form relationships. In 2 Corinthians 6:11-18, Paul taught the church at Corinth to separate themselves from unbelievers and to allow God to become their true source.

*You do not need others to provide for you
what only God is capable of providing!*

The Cost of Accepting your New Father

If God is truly your Father, then you must begin to behave like Him. God is love therefore we must treat others with love, even when and if they are the ones who have hurt us. Remember, we have inherited certain traits and characteristics from our earthly father; some that are positive and some that are negative. Likewise, if Jesus is our father, we should inherit His traits and characteristics, and thank God they are ALL positive.

Self-Reflective Moment

- Write down some of the traits and characteristics you inherited from your earthly father figure.
- Now write down some of the traits and characteristics you inherited from your Heavenly Father.
- Ask yourself this question: How can I use the traits and characteristics from my Heavenly Father to help me to overcome the brokenness I suffer because of the traits and characteristics of my earthly father or other father figures?

How can one accept a new father?

- Accept Jesus Christ as Lord and Savior. - Romans 10:9-10
- Study the Word so you can get to know and develop a relationship with your new Father.
- Develop faith so you can begin to trust your new Father.
- Continue to heal from the hurts and disappointments associated with your earthly father figure to discontinue comparing him to your Heavenly Father.

- Gain an understanding of possible explanations for your earthly father figure's behavior.
- Stop blaming yourself for his shortcomings.
- Forgive your earthly father figure and other male figures in your life that have hurt you.
- Stop playing the victim role.
- Remember, no one is perfect including you.

Why is it so Difficult to Forgive?

It is difficult to forgive when you are not spiritually connected to God in a real way. When we are connected to God, the Holy Spirit will not allow us to maintain unforgiveness. It is also difficult to forgive because we do not want people to think they are off the hook for what they have done to us.

Why is it Necessary to Forgive?

- To please God
- To free ourselves
- To pave the way for healthy relationships
- To live a healthier life
- To be a Christian witness
- To reap bountiful blessings

Consequences of Unforgiveness

- It will make you sick.

- It will make those around you sick.

- It makes God sick.

- You will be unforgiven.

Spiritual Nugget

Let's look at a story of forgiveness found in Genesis 37; 50:14-26

Forgiving versus Forgetting

You will not forget what happened to you, but forgiving means releasing the person from acts of vengeance and making the declaration that you will not allow it to hurt you anymore. So rather than remembering the act or deed, how about focusing on the life lessons you learned from the experience.

Self-Reflection Moment

After spending time talking with your Heavenly Father, write a letter to your earthly father or a male that raised you (even if he was not in your life). This letter should contain the following:

1. The positive impact your father had on your life (even if he was not around).

2. The things that have disappointed you about your father (include your hurt and pain statements here).

3. Talk to your father about what you missed by not having him or having his participation in your life.

4. Let him know what he missed by not participating in your life, if applicable.

5. If you can, allow yourself to write a forgiveness statement at the close of your letter for your earthly father figure(s).

Keeping it Real Testimony!

I had written my biological father off as a loser. Thanks to Keeping it Real, I am willing to consider him as a person who didn't have the tools to raise a "princess" because he did not know how to act like a king. I pray he learns to live a royal life. F.H.

For you have not received the spirit of bondage again to fear, but you have received the Spirit of adoption, whereby we cry, Abba, Father. The Spirit itself bears witness with our Spirit, that we are the children of God.

Romans 8:15-16

Chapter Six

Develop the Mind of Christ

I beseech you therefore, brethren, by the mercies of God, that you present your bodies a living sacrifice, holy, acceptable to God, which is your reasonable service. And do not be conformed to this world, but be transformed by the renewing of your mind, that you may prove what is that good and acceptable and perfect will of God. Romans 12:1-2 KNJV

A few years ago, I attended a very exciting women's conference. There were over 1000 women in attendance, and each speaker worked diligently to motivate the attendees to walk in their purpose and to live a more prosperous and healthy lifestyle. As I scanned the large meeting room, I could not help but wonder what percentage of the attendees would actually make life long changes as a result of what they heard at the conference. I am convinced that some of the ladies, with the help of God and their own dedication and commitment to change, would begin to live a more victorious life. But sadly, I am also convinced that a fair number of the women in attendance would go back to their old way of thinking as soon as they returned home. In fact, some would revert back to old thinking and bad habits on the way to the parking lot. In order for one to become healthy, one must change one's old way of thinking, change bad habits, and develop a Godly mindset. The Scripture teaches: *Let this mind be in you that was also in Christ Jesus"* Philippians 2:5.

Far too many women of God are unhealthy because of negative thinking. The mind is very complex, and when our thinking is negative, it impacts every facet of our lives in negative ways. Belinda, a 46-year old stay at home wife and mother, was asked by the leadership team of her church to serve as a care counselor for the Care Ministry. Belinda had early plans of becoming a counselor before dropping out of college to marry and raise her daughter, so this proposition was quite appealing. However, she refused to accept the assignment.

Belinda's reason for refusing to serve was somewhat perplexing to her pastor, because she stated: "I have to decline this important ministry opportunity because I will not do a good job at it." The pastor was taken back because she possessed several qualities of a good counselor, and people both in and outside the church confided in her all the time. What could be stopping this gifted woman of God from pursuing her purpose with passion? It may have been her level of *Stinking Thinking*.

What is Stinking Thinking?

Stinking thinking is a term used to describe negative thinking that corrupts the entire mind, body, and spirit. We all are guilty of stinking thinking but some bask and dwell in it. It corrodes their very being, and if someone says the sky is beautiful and blue, these persons would have a negative outlook on the situation by saying *it looks dark to me*. The mind is a powerful tool, and our thinking plays a significant impact on how we appraise situations, events, and people.

The mind also impacts one's feelings and behaviors. For example, when you hear a certain song, it can evoke either feelings of joy or sadness. If you associate the song with negative events, you will begin to feel sad upon hearing the song. On the other hand, if you associate the song with positive and uplifting situations, events, and people, you will begin to experience feelings of joy.

What is the Problem with Stinking Thinking?

Stinking thinking is a problem for a variety of reasons:

1. It makes us at-risk of experiencing poor mental, physical, and spiritual health.
2. It interferes with our ability to successfully reach and set goals.
3. It increases the likelihood of poor decision making.
4. It increases the likelihood that we will surround ourselves with other negative thinkers.

5. It contributes to the development of a bad attitude, bad habits, and bad behaviors.

6. It hinders our walk with the Lord and our service to others.

7. It is a demonstration of spiritual immaturity.

How Did I Become So Negative?

I had to really give this question serious thought. How did I become so negative? I realize now that everyone engages in negative thinking at one time or another in one's lifetime. However, people who live in this condition on a daily basis are extremely at-risk of becoming sick in every area. May I keep it real? Sadly, I was one of those persons who was sick much too often. Unexplained headaches, stomach pain, and knots in my stomach, and the doctor never found anything wrong. I was afraid to go to school, so I made every negative excuse to prevent me from going, such as "I'm not smart enough," I can't go to school with a child," and the negative thinking was endless. I did not have a healthy mindset and I continued to hold myself hostage from the past, believing that I was unworthy of being successful.

In addition to the mistakes we make, the guilt we harbor, and our own negative self-perception, there are a number of other possible explanations for negative thinking. For example, when one is born into a family environment filled with negativity, it is highly likely that those living in that environment will also become negative. Therefore, family of origin issues can play a big role in the way we think. Further, past trauma brought on by abuse and abandonment can certainly contribute to a negative mindset. Those who go through a difficult divorce and/or separation can experience mental suffering, especially if the break-up was bad. Unresolved grief and loss issues and sudden mental and physical health challenges can also contribute to destructive thinking. However, one of the most significant factors that contribute to our state of negativity is one's spiritual disconnection from God.

Spiritual Nuggets

What happened to Job's thinking in Job 23:13?

Self-Reflection Moment

- Have you ever experienced a traumatic or uncomfortable situation?
- What were your thoughts, feelings, and behaviors?
- How did you survive?

What are the Benefits of Negative Thinking?

The reason many of us tend to maintain negative thinking is the perceived benefits we enjoy because of it. I know you are asking yourself, how can negativity have any benefits? Well if you really think about it, some of the harmful and destructive thoughts, feelings, and behaviors we engage in are sometimes rationalized and embraced for some of the following reasons:

- We think we can protect ourselves from further hurt.
- We have grown accustomed to this way of thinking so we are in a place of familiarity and temporary comfort.
- We have moved into self-righteousness.
- It helps to maintain anger and bitterness, and is an excuse for unforgiveness.

The Impact of Negative Thinking on Feelings and Behaviors

Aaron Beck, a noted psychologist believed that one's thoughts impact one's feelings and behaviors. He entitled this concept, *The Cognitive Triad*. Further, Beck believed that the way in which one appraises situations and events can have either a positive or negative effect on the way one thinks, feels, and behaves.

Take for example the woman whose husband walks out on her. This would be a terrible situation for anyone, but in this example, the woman appraises the situation as the end of the world. Her negative appraisal of this situation may be influenced by past trauma, which in turn results in negative thinking such as, *I deserve it, I am unattractive, it's all my fault, I am unworthy, etc.* This broken vessel allowed herself to be victimized by her situation, and causing her to experience feelings of sadness and depression brought on by negative thinking, which ultimately impacted her behavior. She is now experiencing suicidal thoughts and behaviors, which is not unusual because of the way in which she appraised the situation in the first place.

You and I will be sick in the mind, body, and spirit with the potential of contaminating others if we fail to modify maladaptive thoughts, feelings, and behaviors. While I do agree with the basic tenets of this interesting theory, I am convinced that failure to develop a Godly mindset will interrupt any long-term changes from taking place in our thinking. Even for those who believe in the power of positive thinking, when tragedy and trauma occur, it is difficult to maintain a positive mindset without the presence of God and the working of the Holy Spirit.

Spiritual Nuggets

1. Read Genesis 16:1-16.

    - How did Sarah appraise her situation?

    - What were Sarah's thoughts?

    - What were her feelings?

    - What were her behaviors?

2. Read Psalms 73.

    - How did Asaph appraise his situation?

    - Where were Asaph's thoughts?

    - What were his behaviors?

3. Read Romans 7:14-24 and 8:1-17.

    - What does the spirit versus the flesh have to do with our thinking?

4. Read I Kings 17:8 and the book of Ruth.

    - What does Faith have to do with our thinking?

Self-Reflection Moment

What are some of the benefits of developing a Godly mindset?

Strategies for Developing a Godly Mindset

There are several important strategies for developing and maintaining a Godly mindset.

1. Make a commitment to develop a Godly mindset and keep it by utilizing the spiritual disciplines of prayer, fasting, praise, and worship. But first, **YOU MUST BE SAVED!** These principles do not apply to those who do not know Jesus Christ as Lord and Savior? *(Romans 10:9-10)* How can you develop a Godly mindset without knowing God? You may not know the mind of Christ, but when you know Him, the Holy Spirit will reveal His plan and prescription for your life. We must love him with our whole heart, mind, and spirit. (*Luke 10:27*)

2. Strive to become spiritually mature, and you will begin to develop wisdom and become better able to understand the mind of Christ. It is the power of God that gives us wisdom. (*I Corinthian 2:1-16*) When we possess the spirit of God we will take on the mind of Christ. Perhaps the reason He has not revealed himself to you at this point in your life, is because you are not ready. It does not matter how well you know the Scripture or how educated and wise you believe you are, without God's spirit, you will fall into the vice grips of negativity.

3.   Develop faith, the kind that was demonstrated in the book of Ruth. Remember, faith without works is dead. *(James 2:17)*

4.   Guard your mind. *(Proverbs 15:13-14)*

5.   Renew your mind. *(Romans 12:1-3)*

6.   Keep your mind stayed on Him. *(Isaiah 26:1)*

7.   Stop worrying, rejoice in the Lord and pray. *(Philippians 4:8)*

8.   Change your environment. *(Matthew 9:16-17)*

9.   Become willing to change bad habits. *(I John 3:8-9)*

10. Exercise Forgiveness. *(Matthew 18:35)*

11. Seek wise counsel and get professional help by a trained Christian therapist if necessary. *(Proverbs 15:22)*

12. Put *Ephesians 4* into practice.

Self-Reflection Moment

- Think about the same situation you shared earlier, and this time modify your thinking, and see what happens to your feelings and behaviors.

- What are some of the things you need to do to change your thinking on a consistent basis?

- Are you willing to make a change?

Keeping it Real Testimony!

I was broken from a marriage that was out of control. I made a conscious decision to forgive myself and my spouse for the betrayal. I continue to renew my mind through daily devotion. I now call on the Holy Spirit to help me to change any "stinking thinking."

For who hath known the mind of the Lord, that he may instruct him? But we have the mind of Christ. I Corinthian 2:16

Chapter Seven

Let the Spirit Control You, Not the Flesh

For if you live according to the flesh you will die; but if by the Spirit you put to death the deeds of the body, you will live. Romans 8:13(NKJV)

I have come a long way in my journey toward healing and wholeness, but I also recognize that I am a work in progress. God still has so much more to teach me. I am well aware that without the Spirit of God in full operation in my life, I will never be totally healthy. As Christian women we must actively strive to discover the keys to enjoying healthy family relationships with spouses, children (both biological and step-children), parents, and siblings.

God impressed upon me, as He usually does when He wants to teach me important lessons, to discuss strategies for developing and maintaining healthy relationships with those we love the most. This is a critical component to one's health and well-being because so many people are sick because of unhealthy relationships with those closest to them. Operating in the Spirit is critical to all aspects of our lives as Christian women. But in this final chapter, we will investigate the significance and benefits of allowing ourselves to be controlled by the Spirit of God as opposed to the flesh in order to live a healthier lifestyle and to have healthier relationships with those we love and care about.

He is Getting on my Nerves

Every couple has challenges in their marital relationship because of one or more of the following factors: excess items in each individual's suitcase, personality differences, cultural differences, blended family issues, financial and communication problems. That's right! No one is exempt. Can I keep it real? My husband is a visionary leader. Not only is he a pastor of a thriving ministry, the man is quite a successful entrepreneur and businessman. He is a great blessing in my life, and I feel very fortunate because every woman wants a true leader, especially when the leader is Godly. Unfortunately, because of the heavy load in my suitcase, and my husband's high tolerance for risk-taking, his strategies for securing the future of our family were sometimes very scary to me. I must keep it real and share with you that I did not always handle the situation in a Godly manner.

Ladies, our husbands have been given the responsibility of taking care of their family. Maybe they have not done what you would have liked in this area, but it is still the intention of real men to provide for their family. Since men and women think and process differently, it is not unlikely that women can experience some level of stress and unrest when decisions are made that they have not participated in, or had the opportunity to discuss before the decisions were made. Nonetheless, we as women of God can find perfect peace in every situation if we simply allow ourselves to be controlled by the Spirit of God and not by the flesh. It has taken me several years to understand and apply this concept, and even now, it is not easy to do, although I know that when I rely on the Holy Spirit there is peace that surpasses all understanding.

I remember my husband sharing an idea he had. It was a great idea, but I could just feel my stomach begin to churn as I thought to myself, "Oh no, not another dream. Why doesn't this man just wake up?" As the anxiety began to build, my thinking became very negative, and I grew angry which was accompanied by a very bad attitude. Gloria was all flesh that night, which happened to be Saturday night. I knew full well that I was wrong in my approach, but I had passed the point of no return. It was of no consequence to me that my beloved husband had to minister the next day, I just wanted to please my flesh. My flesh was leading every thought, feeling, and behavior, and I had the nerve to hop in the car the next day for church. I was waiting for him to say something so I could let him have it.

This particular Sunday, a guest speaker spoke at our church, and it seemed as though the message was written and spoken with me in mind. Has God ever spoken to you through a sermon, song, or prayer? Well that day, it was my turn. I felt so convicted, not because I was totally wrong in my concerns, but because I allowed my flesh to take control of the situation in order to reduce my anxiety. *Ladies, the flesh will never be able to relieve you of what is ailing you.* I am beginning to learn that it really does not matter if you are correct in your thinking about the situation; you and I are still responsible for our actions.

I could hardly wait for the altar call so I could ask my husband to forgive me for the behavior I exhibited toward him. So at that very moment, in front of God and the waiting congregation, I humbled myself and apologized to my husband. It was a great day for our church, because so many people were also convicted because of their bad behavior toward one another.

Notice I did not place all the blame on the enemy as we are so accustomed to doing. Yes, he always contributes to the situation by edging us on, but we make a conscious decision to respond inappropriately.

Lessons to be Learned

There were so many lessons to be learned that day. First, I learned a great deal more about submission. This is a word that we do not want to use because it suggests that we are allowing ourselves to be oppressed or dominated. I had to learn that when I submit to my husband, I am being obedient to God. In fact, through submission to your spouse, you demonstrate your trust and faith in God. In my clinical practice, I routinely share with couples that they cannot trust each other, because each of them will yield to the flesh far too often. But they can always trust God and the Spirit of God that resides in each of them when they submit to the Holy Spirit.

In the book of Esther, Queen Vashti also had a difficult time submitting to the request of her husband. Be careful ladies! Are you really sure you are ready for the consequences of your disobedience? King Ahasuerus asked Queen Vashti to come to the party wearing her royal crown so he could show her beauty off to the people and the officials. Some may say that the King was exhibiting sexist behavior, and the Queen had a right to refuse his request. Well, she refused to come and her act of disobedience to the King was a source of shame and disgrace. Needless to say, the consequences of her actions were quite severe.

Spiritual Nuggets

In the first chapter of the book of Esther, what were the consequences of Queen Vashti's response to her husband?

The other lesson I learned was the importance of making a Godly response in every situation, crisis, or calamity, regardless of whether you are right or wrong. The only way we are able to do this is to kill the flesh daily.

Spiritual Nuggets

Read Esther 1:17 to gain a better understanding of why her disobedience was so distasteful to the King.

What About the Children?

Another area of difficulty and challenge for women is the area of child rearing, whether raising biological or step children. Few women become a parent totally equipped and skilled for the job. Therefore, the parenting skills we did or did not develop are based on what we experienced from our parents and/or caregivers, books, or television. Far too often women of God struggle in this area, especially when they are single parents trying to play the role of mother and father. Sometimes the father is in the home yet he may be disengaged from the parental process. It is especially important for mothers, regardless of your circumstances to operate in the Spirit of God as you attempt to parent, because this job is far too hard for you alone.

Further, some are in the step-mother role, which can be very difficult and complicated. However, it is even more difficult if the biological father and mother have been unable to settle their differences, or the new couple is in a bad marital relationship.

Parenting is also more difficult when the parents do not agree on parenting styles. Lois was the mother of 3 children, one 15-year old daughter and 2 sons, ages 10 and 11. She and her husband had been married 20 years. Each of them possessed different ideas about parenting. Lois was raised in a strict Christian home with both her parents, and her husband Walter grew up in a single female headed household that had fewer rules and restrictions. Her parenting style was much more rigid and structured and his parenting style was much more permissive.

Lois and Walter fought all the time over the children, and it was apparent that the children began to manipulate the situation for their good. Lois was very angry and upset most of the time, especially over the way her husband was disengaged with his sons. These fights over the children soon began to interfere with the quality of their marital relationship, and the couple was on the brink of divorce. Both Lois and Walter were Christians and after counseling they were able to seek God's guidance and learned how to apply spiritual principles to every situation, including their marriage and raising their children. Basically, they learned the importance of walking in the Spirit and lethal consequences of walking in the flesh.

> ## *Self-Reflection Moment*
> Why is it so difficult for me to walk in the Spirit instead of the flesh?

It Feels Sooo Good

I can say with all assurance that when I allow the Spirit of God to take control of my life, I am at peace with myself and others. But can I keep it real? That peaceful condition is sometimes short lived because we fail to do the work required to wear our Spiritual garments more often. We are then more likely to be controlled by the flesh. As you know, you and I will do whatever the flesh wants. In Romans 7 and 8, Paul admonished us to walk in the Spirit and not in the flesh. Failure to walk in the Spirit leads to faulty decision making, which can result in long-term negative consequences.

Just go to the mall on a window shopping excursion. There you will see the perfect pair of shoes and they only cost $300.00. Now you know those shoes are outside your budget, and buying them will create even greater problems, but you must have them because you must satisfy the flesh even if the Spirit is saying DON'T DO IT!

Can you remember the time someone said something that offended you and the flesh helped you to recall and use words you promised you would never speak again? It feels sooo good, but the pleasure does not last long.

When we are hurting and broken, we tend to attempt to gain power over our lives by satisfying the flesh. However, if we are going to regain power and strength, we can only accomplish that goal by overcoming the control of the flesh and allow ourselves to be controlled by the Spirit of God.

Remember, there will always be a battle between the flesh and the Spirit, so prepare spiritually for the fight!

Strategies for Killing the Flesh

- Become spiritually mature by studying God's Word, prayer, fasting, praise, worship, and fellowshipping with other believers.
- Acknowledge your brokenness and identify and strive to eliminate destructive forms of self-medication, such as drinking, overeating, illicit sexual behaviors, excessive shopping, and gambling.
- Embrace the concept of denying yourself and obeying God.
- Understand that killing the flesh is a daily activity.
- Forgive those who have hurt you, including yourself.
- Read Romans Chapters 7 and 8.

Self-Reflection Moment

You may be allowing yourself to be controlled by the flesh, which can only result in Spiritual death. What will you commit to do to kill the flesh and become controlled by the Spirit of God?

Keeping it Real Testimony!

It is my intention to spiritually fortify myself so that I can be a blessing to the body of Christ rather than a hindrance. J.J.

A PROMISE BY THE MASTER

If you love me, keep my commandments, and I will pray the Father, and He will give you another Helper that He may abide with you forever- The Spirit of truth whom the world cannot receive, because it neither sees him nor knows Him; but you know Him, for He dwells with you and will be in you. I will not leave you orphans; I will come to you. A little while longer and the world will see Me no more, but you will see Me. Because I live, you will live also. At that day you will know that I am in My Father, and you in Me, and I in you. He who has my commandments and keeps them, it is he who loves me. And he who loves Me will be loved by my Father, and I will love him and manifest Myself to him."　　　　　　　　　　　*John 14:15-21*

Epilogue

Living My Life Like its Golden

For whatever is born of God overcomes the world. And this is the victory that has overcome the world – our faith. I John 5:4 NKJV

I heard a song the other day by popular artist Jill Scott, and one of the verses says:

I'm holding onto my freedom, can't take it from me, I was born into it, and it comes naturally. I'm strumming my own freedom, playing the God in me, Representing His glory, hope He's proud of me! Living my life like its golden, hope He's proud of me.

These lyrics represent my new mantra, with one exception. I know beyond a shadow of a doubt that my Heavenly Father is proud of me. I have certainly come a long way, even though I have a long way to go. I am now living my life like its golden because that is the life God has designed me to live. I must admit, however, that there are times when I slip back into my old way of thinking, which is an inevitable reality for an imperfect human being. The difference is, I have learned some of the secrets to living a healthier and purpose driven life, which I have had the pleasure of sharing with you in this book. It is my prayer that you too have discovered some of the secrets to a healthier you, and that you will begin to live your life like its golden.

There is Purpose in your Suffering

No matter what you have been through, or what you are currently going through, God wants you to know there is purpose in your suffering. It took many years for me to reveal my own suicide attempt because it became another source of shame and guilt that I had to recover from. I was afraid that others would judge me or try to convince me that I was not saved. But God allowed me to go through that dark time in my life so I would be able to relate to the pain and suffering of others.

The work He has called me to do, requires me to sit with people who have either thought of harming themselves or have made actual attempts. Who could better minister to them than someone who has been there? Let me keep it real! Every powerful man and woman of God in the bible experienced great human suffering. Therefore, do not allow your suffering to prevent you from doing the great work God has ordained you to do.

Spiritual Nuggets

And we know that all things work together for good to them that love God, to them who are the called according to His purpose. Romans 8:28

Here's To A Healthier You!

The fact that you have come to this page in the book, just might suggest that you are well on your way to becoming healthier and whole. What should the healthier you look like?

- The healthier you can acknowledge your condition and get the necessary mental, physical, and spiritual help to recover.
- The healthier you can write down your dream/vision for your life and pursue your purpose with passion.
- The healthier you can set and reach realistic personal, professional, and spiritual goals.
- The healthier you can acknowledge that you are imperfect and prone to fall, but have confidence that you SHALL rise again.
- The healthier you can help others to become healthier.
- The healthier you WILL live your life like its golden and stop living in the past.

Living in the past may cause paralysis that can prevent one from successfully walking toward the future. Gloria Morrow, 2004

Self-Affirmation

Take a moment to think about your progress. You certainly have accomplished a lot by being dutiful to this process of becoming healthier. Write those accomplishments on a piece of paper, and affirm yourself for reaching this point in your journey. Be sure to celebrate yourself and give all glory to God.

Keeping it Real Testimony!

I am even more focused on living a life that will please the Lord. V.R.

He that hath an ear, let him hear what the Spirit saith unto the churches; To him that overcometh will I give to eat of the tree of life, which is in the midst of the paradise of God.   *Revelation 2:7*

RESOURCES

These resources may be helpful to you, a family member or friend.

American Psychological Association

750 First Street, NE

Washington D.C. 20002-4242

(800) 374-2721

www.apa.org

Association of Black Psychologists (ABPSI)

P.O. Box 55999

Washington D.C. 20040-5999

(202) 722-0808

www.abpsi.org

Black Psychiatrist of America

C/o Ramona Davis, M.D.

866 Carlston Avenue

Oakland, CA 94610

(510) 834-7103

www.blackpsychiatristofamerica.com

National Alliance for the Mentally Ill

Colonial Place Three

2107 Wilson Blvd., Ste. 300

Arlington, VA 22201

1-800-950-NAMI or 703-524-7600

www.nami.org

National Black Women's Health Project

600 Pennsylvania Avenue SE, Suite 310

Washington DC 20003

(202) 548-4000

www.nationalblackwomenshealthproject.org

National Domestic Violence Hotline

800-799-7233

National Institute of Mental Health (NIMH)

5600 Fishers Lane, Room 7-99

Rockville, MD 20857

(888) ANXIETY

www.nimh.nih.gov/anxiety

National Mental Health Association

1021 Prince Street

Alexandria, VA 22314-2971

(800) 969-nmha

www.nmha.org

National Suicide Hotline

1-800-SUICIDE

Rape, Abuse, Incest National Network

800 656-HOPE

INTERNET SOURCES

www.blackhealth.com

www.blackwomenshealth.org/site/PageServer

www.cabwhp.org

www.census.gov

www.healthyplace.com/communities/depression/minorities_9asp

www.hopeallianz.com/ResourceCenter/Suicide6_warningsigns.html

www.mentalhealth.org/cre/ch3_historical_context.asp. Minorities &
Mental Health Report of the U.S. Surgeon General

www.mentalhealth.org/cre/fact1.asp

www.psychologytoday.com/htdocs/prod/PTOArticle/PTO-20030930-
000001.asp. Psychology Today's Blues Buster Newsletter
(September 30, 2003)

www.womensenews.org/article.cfm/dyn/aid/1392/context/archive

SELECTED BIBLIOGRAPHY

Beck, A.T. (1976) Cognitive therapy and the emotional disorders.
New York: International Universities Press.

Hudson, H.M. & Stern, H.(2000). The heart of the matter. Roscoe, Il.:
Hilton Publishing.

Life Application Bible (1989) King James Version, Tyndale
House Pub.

Martin, M. (2002). Saving our last nerve. Roscoe, Il: Hilton Publication

Maxmen, J.S. & Ward,N.G. (1995). Essential psychopathology and its
treatment, (2nd ed.), New York, NY: W.W. Norton & Co. (p.219)

Morrow, G. (2003). Too broken to be fixed? A spiritual guide to inner
healing. Pomona, CA: Shining Glory Publications, Inc.

Morrow, G. (2005). Strengthening the Ties that Bind: A guide to a healthy
marriage. Pomona, CA: Shining Glory Publications, Inc.

Neal-Barnett, A. (2003). Soothe your nerves: The Black woman's guide
to understanding and overcoming anxiety, panic, & fear. New
York, N.Y.: Simon & Shuster.

Omartian, S. (1997). The power of a praying wife. Oregon: Harvest
House Pubishers.

Plomin, R. (1994). Genetics and experience: The interplay between
nature and nurture. Newbury Park, CA: Sage

SELECTED BIBLIOGRAPHY

Queener, J.E., & Martin, J.K. (2001). Providing culturally relevant mental health services: Collaboration between psychology and the African American church. Journal of Black Psychology, 27, 1, 112-122.

Warren, R. (2002). The purpose driven life. Grand Rapids, Mi: Zondervan.

Additional Books by
Dr. Gloria Morrow

Too Broken To Be Fixed?: A Spiritual Guide To Inner Healing

By Dr. Gloria Morrow

Dr. Morrow addresses the issue of depression in the African/American community and the role of the faith community in responding to this issue.

Strengthening the Ties that Bind: A guide to a healthy marriage

By Dr. Gloria Morrow

Dr. Morrow discusses some of the challenges that married couples face as well as strategies for strengthening their marriages.

The book contains activities for couples to help them to begin the process of healing their marital relationships.

The Things That Make Men Cry

By Dr. Gloria Morrow

Dr. Morrow conducted extensive and intimate interviews with 20 men who share their stories of manhood and fatherhood, and the things they want to say to their women. These brave men explore and discuss the issues that make them, and other men cry both internally and externally.

Products may be purchased by visiting www.gloriamorrow.com.

Personal Reflections

_____

_____

_____

_____

_____

_____

_____

_____

Personal Reflections

_____

_____

_____

_____

_____

_____

_____

_____

Personal Reflections

Keeping It Real!
∞